"*Don't Just Send a Resume* should be required reading for all seminary students and job-seeking pastors! As one who has hired 1,800+ staff in a professional career, my radar was 'on' to see how the author would treat the big concepts and the gritty details. He nailed it for me! 'Thank God for Benjamin Vrbicek!' may become a common praise uttered by ministry jobseekers throughout the US."

Tim Beltz
Retired Captain (USCG); retired executive pastor; church consultant; and author of *Charting the Course*

"After studying in seminary and working in seminary admissions, I see a great need for Benjamin's book. There is nothing else like it! I will recommend it to men who are called to ministry, regardless of their denomination."

Timothy Brindle
Hip-hop recording artist; author of *The Unfolding*; and Senior Admissions Counselor, Westminster Theological Seminary

"Exceptional writing. The main themes are introduced and expounded. *Don't Just Send a Resume* has a strong biblical basis to it as well as concrete advice. A pastor can read this and know just what to do."

Jeff Davis
Director of Child Evangelism Fellowship of Eastern PA, Inc.; Adjunct Professor at Capital Bible Seminary & Graduate School and Liberty University

"If you aspire to pastoral ministry, you don't have to look too hard for bad advice. So much of it is either presumptuous or impractical. Thankfully, with *Don't Just Send a Resume*, Benjamin Vrbicek has written a book that's neither. Pick it up, read it, and profit from his hard-won wisdom."

Alex Duke
Managing Editor for 9Marks

"I still remember the frustration, pain, and confusion I felt as a young, aspiring pastor right out of seminary looking for the perfect church. Now I am on the other side helping aspiring missionaries and church planters discern God's calling and timing for ministry placement. This book will be a great encouragement and practical help to anyone pursuing full-time ministry."

Scott Dunford
Vice President at ABWE International; co-host of *The Missions* podcast

"Benjamin Vrbicek's *Don't Just Send a Resume* is a thorough and systematic guide for any pastor seeking to move to another ministry. Benjamin's book is biblically grounded, principled, and true to the minister's experiences while aptly answering the *hows* and *whys* of seeking to serve in another corner of God's kingdom. It has proven to be a great tool for this seasoned pastor."

Paulo Freire
Pastor of Hope Evangelical Free Church, Wantage, NJ

"Benjamin writes on this subject with a personal transparency, theological richness, and attention to detail that is really compelling. As a lay elder who has led a couple pastoral search committees, I found the book accessible, helpful, and practical, and though it was not written for this purpose, I would use it as a reference if I was called on to lead another committee. I highly recommend the book to you."

Michael Grenier

Manager at TE Connectivity; lay-elder; and veteran of pastoral search committees

"Don't Just Send a Resume is a gift for those starting out in pastoral ministry. It will not only answer 'how-to' questions about searching for a ministry position, but it will also help you do so with the right expectations and the right heart. I can see readers reaching for this valuable resource throughout the entire job-search process. I wish I read this book as a seminary student!"

Kevin Halloran

Content Strategist and Trainer with Leadership Resources International

"In my fifteen years of work with vocational ministry placement, two facts have been consistent. First, search committees need help. Second, ministry candidates need guidance. This book addresses the second, offering practical direction on issues widely applicable to the ministry candidating process. The questions are practical. The situations are real. The insights are poignant. I use this book in my seminary course on candidating, and I recommend it to all pastors considering a new ministry position."

Joel D. Hathaway

Director of Alumni & Career Services, Covenant Theological Seminary; author of *Finding a Pastor: A Handbook for Ministerial Search Committees*

"Benjamin Vrbicek combines the heart of a pastor with the savviness of a recruiter. With great conversational style, he provides the great gift of insightful, practical advice into the job-search process—a topic that can be woefully under-addressed for those entering the ministry. It's a valuable book from an insightful leader."

Eric Herrenkohl

Business Consultant and author of *How to Hire A-Players*

"As a district staff member with the EFCA, I help pastors and churches in their placement. Sometimes it is like a hand in glove fit, but often it can be an arduous game of putting your best foot forward—prayer, sweat, wait and see. Benjamin Vrbicek has masterfully woven the threads of pitfalls and fears of looking for a job along with offering wise counsel for finding the proper fit as a pastor in a new church. This book should be read by every pastor looking for a new ministry position."

Peter Johnson

Associate District Superintendent of the Eastern District of the Evangelical Free Church of America

"As pastors we are taught to faithfully handle God's Word and shepherd his people and not be self-promoters in a job-search process. I'm grateful for the practical help this book offers, but I'm more grateful for the heart behind all the words. This process can be hard emotionally and spiritually and can impact your family and marriage. Benjamin seeks to pastor other pastors as they engage in their own process of seeking God's calling and placement."

Simon Kim
Associate Pastor of Desert Hills Presbyterian Church, Scottsdale, AZ

"Finding the right person for local church ministry positions is a challenge for both potential candidates and church leadership. Potential candidates are looking for a role that fits their unique gifts and abilities, while local church leaders are looking for the person the Lord has uniquely prepared for their church context. Too many times, complications arise unnecessarily due to a lack of understanding of a healthy search process. Benjamin Vrbicek has given an incredible gift to candidates and committees in his book *Don't Just Send a Resume*. This book is filled with wise advice and practical tips that will give great help to those navigating the ministry search process. I highly recommend it!"

Kevin Kompelien
President of the Evangelical Free Church of America

"This book is fantastic! I will heartily recommend it to my sphere of influence as required reading. I love Benjamin's writing. In fact, I just finished reading the chapter on money to my wife. We thought it was excellent!"

Keith Krell
Senior Pastor of Crossroads Bible Church, Bellevue, WA; coauthor of *Paul and Money*

"I'm thankful for Benjamin, his writing ministry, and this new book in particular. Here he wisely shepherds Christian leaders through some of the most important transitions we will ever make. It's grounded, sensitive, and exceptionally helpful."

Jeremy Linneman
Lead Pastor of Trinity Community Church, Columbia, MO; author of *Life-Giving Groups*

"Anyone looking for a 'job' in a local church will want to read this book, and all of us who already have found one will wish we had it back then. With his happy, humorous, and friendly writer's voice, Benjamin Vrbicek deftly blends the relevant theological truths with truly helpful tips for making the most of the search process from the candidate's end. I keep giving away copies to my friends."

Matthew Mitchell
Pastor of Lanse Evangelical Free Church, Lanse, PA; author of *Resisting Gossip*

"This is the book that every seminary student needed to read and didn't get to. Simple and practical yet detailed and insightful, this will serve as a great go-to guide for pursuing a new position in ministry, whether it be the first call or a later one. Most importantly, this book helps the pastor consider the entire process through a biblical framework."

Stephen Morefield
Pastor of Christ Covenant EPC, Leoti, KS; author of *Fierce Grace*

"Benjamin's prose is clean and engaging. I love the overall gospel foundation that undergirds this book and the practical focus that stems out of it. I think it could be helpful to people!"

Gavin Ortlund
Pastor of First Baptist Church of Ojai, Ojai, CA; author and popular blogger

"The search committee process can be brutal for pastors and their families. This book is a lifeline, providing *both* the practical 'how-tos' as well as an essential gospel-undergirding. The foundation of *Don't Just Send a Resume* is trust in the goodness and sovereignty of God and from there Benjamin offers invaluable wisdom and insight—he's thought of everything! A must-read for future seminary graduates or transitioning pastors."

Jen Oshman
Former overseas missionary; pastor's wife; popular blogger; and author of a forthcoming book with Crossway

"Applying for a job as a pastor can be a strange and disorienting process. It can feel like the means used to land the job—working your connections, crafting a personal brand, positioning for a vote—are the very things you'll want to preach against your first Sunday in the pulpit. Benjamin's book serves as a trusted friend to help you keep hold of God in the process. Practical, wise, and well written, I don't know of any other book as valuable during your transitions."

Chase Replogle
Pastor of Bent Oak Church, Springfield, MO; host of the *Pastor Writer* podcast

"What does the gospel have to do with how we seek a job? The author and contributors of this unique volume answer this very question, and the result is a book that will help readers transition in a way that is faithful to the 1 Corinthians 10:31 mandate. Whether you're new to the ministry and seeking your first ministry position or you're pastoring those who are or will be in such circumstances, this book will give you biblical guidance and will also build up your soul."

Jeff Robinson
Senior Editor for The Gospel Coalition; Lead Pastor of Christ Fellowship Church, Louisville, KY

"In this book, Vrbicek does something astonishing: he makes the ministry job hunt feel survivable. He places a hand on your shoulder and guides you through the woods with an assurance that only comes from ample experience on both sides of the hiring process. For job hunters already drowning in abstract advice that fits other professions but has little bearing on ministry employment, this book is refreshingly practical and ministry-specific—all meat, no grizzle. This is the survival guide I would want on my nightstand if I were facing the church job market for the first time or reentering it after years of steady work."

Kyle Rohane

Managing Editor for CTPastors.com and BuildingChurchLeaders.com

"Practical, informative, and encouraging. Highly recommended for new and established ministers."

Quentin Schultze

Professor Emeritus at Calvin College; author of many books including *Communicate Like a True Leader, Résumé 101*, and *Habits of the High-Tech Heart*

"Benjamin's book is full of practical wisdom, and I highly recommend it. As a pastor recently looking for a church position, I didn't know what questions to ask in my search. Benjamin provided me with helpful advice and also with the reassurance that I'm not alone in this process—others have navigated these waters before me."

Dustin Tramel

Associate Pastor of Redeemer Church, London, England

"The process of finding a church home to minister in is one of the more difficult things about pastoral ministry. The process is long and arduous. Benjamin Vrbicek's book is filled with theological and practical help for the pastor who is searching."

Jason Worsley

Preaching Pastor of Grace Bible Church, Grapevine, TX

"*Don't Just Send a Resume* is a needed resource, and it is a helpful resource. It is needed because I simply am not aware of another book tackling this specific issue that is so common in ministry. It is helpful because the author has labored to provide pastoral and practical advice. I can see myself taking all my staff through this book to prepare them for the eventual day they transition from one church to another church."

Scott Zeller

Executive Pastor of Redeemer Church of Dubai, Dubai, U.A.E.

Don't Just Send a Resume

HOW TO FIND THE RIGHT
JOB IN A LOCAL CHURCH

DON'T *Just* SEND A RESUME

BENJAMIN VRBICEK

CONTRIBUTIONS BY

Chris Brauns | Cara Croft | Dave Harvey | David Mathis | J. A. Medders | Sam Rainer
Chase Replogle | William Vanderbloemen | Kristen Wetherell | Jared C. Wilson | Jeremy Writebol

Don't Just Send a Resume: How to Find the Right Job in a Local Church
by Benjamin Vrbicek

Cover design: Matt Higgins
Interior design: Benjamin Vrbicek

A publication of FAN AND FLAME Press in Harrisburg, PA

Hardback ISBN: 978-0997570236
Trade paperback ISBN: 978-0997570243
Ebook ISBN: 978-0997570267

Special thanks to Jason Abbott, Mary Wells, Ben Bechtel, Russell Meek, Stacey Covell, Alex Duke, Alexandra Richter, and dozens of early readers for their editorial assistance.

A few notes about citations. *First*, for the sake of confidentiality, quotations from personal interviews are intentionally not attributed to the respective pastors. *Second*, contributions from some authors have been adapted with permission from articles previously published online: Sam Rainer ("Early Discernment at the Beginning of God's Call," *SamRainer.com*, April 25, 2013), Kevin DeYoung ("7 Common Mistakes Search Committees Make," *The Gospel Coalition,* July 7, 2016), William Vanderbloemen ("3 Temptations That Can Trick You into Taking the Wrong Church Job," *Vanderbloemen.com*, February 9, 2015), and Dave Harvey ("What's the Best Way for a Pastor to Negotiate His Salary?" *AmICalled.com*, March 2017). *Third*, a few previously published articles by Benjamin Vrbicek were adapted for this book. They do not receive footnotes in the text but are as follows: Introduction, pp. 1–5 ("Am I Still Me? Finding Yourself When Life Changes," *Desiring God*, April 18, 2017), chapter 6, pp. 82–84 ("Pastor, Strive to Learn Their Names," *The Gospel Coalition*, September 11, 2017), chapter 7, pp. 95–106 ("Pastoral Transplant Criteria," *For The Church*, December 26, 2015), and chapter 11, pp. 152–55 ("Pastors Need Healthy Boundaries," *Evangelical Free Church of America Eastern District Blog*, January 18, 2017).

Scripture quotations are from The ESV® Bible (The Holy Bible, English Standard Version®), copyright © 2001 by Crossway, a publishing ministry of Good News Publishers. 2016 Text Edition. Used by permission. All rights reserved.

All emphases in Scripture quotations have been added by the author.

To New Life Bible Fellowship
for taking a risk on a rookie pastor
whose calling was clear but gifts were raw

CONTENTS

Contributors

It took me five years to earn my seminary degree. It was exhausting. It cost thousands of dollars and took thousands of hours to learn what I needed to learn so I could help lead a local church. Eventually that training was complete, and it was time for my classmates and me to look for jobs.

This didn't go well for many of us. In fact, some students—men I respect and thought would make great pastors—struggled to find the right church or any church at all.

In a word, they floundered.

Why? Because they didn't know how to find a job. They didn't know what they were doing. I suspect there are valid reasons why this was the case.

First, they forgot—or they never learned—that the business world is different from the vocational ministry world. These differences startled me when I began interviewing for pastoral jobs. For example, during the interview process with one church, the pastors visited my home for a meal. They met my entire family and even saw my laundry room during a tour of our house. Trust me, this never happened during my former career as a mechanical engineer.

Second, pastors struggle to connect with the right local church because many seminaries don't have margin to teach students how to transition from the classroom. For every book a professor includes, there are ten others he or she wanted to add but couldn't.

If you're a seminary student about to graduate, it's no guarantee you'll have a pastoral job in a few months. You know the feeling—and it's terrifying. In his book to help pastors during transitions, John Cionca writes, "Occasionally, I meet seminarians who view a Master of Divinity degree as a union card. They figure that someone owes them a church upon graduation."[1] I'm not sure I'd go this far, but I understand the sentiment. All that effort, time, and money—in addition to a sense of calling that's been confirmed by others—creates certain expectations, or at least certain hopes.

So, when the end of the tunnel starts to look more hopeless than hopeful, disillusionment and panic ensue. It's overwhelming to think about all the steps involved in finding the right job, especially if you've never done it before. *Where do I start? Who do I talk to? What do I send them?* It's no less terrifying when you're currently in a church but considering a new role. *How do I know my family and I will fit at the new church? How do I tell people I'm leaving?*

For all those questions, we pastors need solid coaching. We need processes that are theologically informed and practically oriented. We need anecdotes from real hiring processes, and we need strategies for every step of the way.[2]

This is what *Don't Just Send a Resume* is about. Consider for a moment an Emergency Medical Technician (EMT). An EMT, though trained, needs an ambulance to get him to the accident. He's been trained to help those who are hurt, but he needs a ride to be able to do so. If he can't get to the accident, he can't help. In the same way, I'm not interested in pastors earning a lot of money or finding the flashiest job. I simply want to get those who are trained to help—pastors—on the path to those churches who need their help.

This whole project started with two e-mails. Joel, a friend from seminary, emailed me to ask for advice about finding a job in a church. That was three and a half years ago. Joel was about to transition from

---

[1] John R. Cionca, *Before You Move: A Guide to Making Transitions in Ministry* (Grand Rapids, MI: Kregel, 2004), 35.

[2] My own theological convictions are complementarian, and because this book is largely directed at pastors, this means I'll often assume I'm speaking to men. However, I also hope the book will help women seeking various ministry roles, including pastoral roles, within churches, as well as help both male and female parachurch leaders and missionaries.

one church to another, and he was looking for help. I sent him an e-mail with ten suggestions. *Who sends a ten-point e-mail?* I guess I do! Anyway, Joel found my thoughts, as well as the subsequent coaching I gave him, helpful. After that, my e-mail to Joel grew into a series of blog posts. Then came eighteen months of research with my nose in books on the topic, both church-specific and business-specific books. Then came over fifty interviews with pastors of all different ages and roles and denominations who'd recently made a pastoral transition. Then I reached out to other pastors and authors who have thought deeply about pastoral transitions, asking them to contribute to the book. And finally, this book—or, rather, this ambulance.

Let's go for a ride.

SET THE PROPER FOUNDATION

Let us be grateful for receiving a kingdom that cannot be shaken.
– Hebrews 12:28

A job search can shake you to the core. For most pastors, it will include rejections and disappointments. Even the successful search can try one's patience. This means pastors must have something at their core that can't be shaken. It means that before we talk about cover letters, resumes, and a host of other important details, we need to talk about identity in Christ, prayer, and the goodness and sovereignty of God.

Don't Reinvent Yourself; Reidentify with Christ

The last thirteen years of my life have been full of transition. I went from single to married; from relying on my parents to being a parent myself; from a classroom to a cubicle and then to a church; from just a little money to lots of money and then to something less than lots of money; and from a Division I college athlete to a less-athletic dad.

And that doesn't even include the eight houses, the five churches in four denominations, the four job changes in four different cities, and going from zero children to six children (with a miscarriage in there as well).

1

Perhaps all this transition explains my sense of vertigo. It's difficult to get your bearings when the world beneath your feet keeps shifting year after year after year.

Transitions in the Bible

The Bible is full of transitions. We move from just two people in a garden to thriving cities; from one man named Abram to the whole nation of Israel; from tribal rulers to mighty kings; from prosperous ease to crippling desolation—and around and around that dizzying Ferris wheel we go. The people of God transition from the intermittent altars used by the patriarchs to the portable tabernacle to the fixed temple and finally to the curtain torn in two.

We also see transitions at the individual level. In the Old Testament, Abram leaves his family, and David goes from a shepherd to a king. In the New Testament, the disciples change from fishermen to church leaders, and untold numbers of sinners become saints.

Consider the upheaval in Moses's life and his three major transitions: from being raised in the family of a foreign king to life as an obscure shepherd and finally to leading the Hebrew people. He knew as much as anyone what it means to be disoriented by transition and change (Exod 3:11).

What's Your Focus in Transitions?

If you're like most people, your life will be full of transitions. Perhaps not to the magnitude of Moses's nor with the frequency of my last decade, but you will experience change.

During these changes you'll be forced to ask and answer good questions like these:

What am I passionate about?
Who am I *now*?
Who do I want to be *later*?
What do I want to be known for?

Your answers will move in one of two very different directions. You could "re-invent yourself." In our culture this typically requires a kind of self-centered and godless exercise. By "godless," I don't mean it's the sum of all evil. I simply mean it provokes us to consider transition without any consideration of God. People look inward, asking, *Who am I?* And they look outward, thinking, I want to be like *these* people and not like *those* people.

Throughout this re-invention process, the unspoken assumption is something like this: Life's outcomes are infinitely malleable, and if *I* try hard enough, then *I* can be whatever *I* want. God is hardly in the picture—it's all inward and outward, not upward.

Thankfully, for the Christian, there's a better option. Christians can use transitions to re-identify with who we are in Christ. They offer an opportunity to reaffirm that the defining reality of our lives is not found in our marital status or our address, our income or our vocation, our looks or our popularity. Our defining reality isn't outward or inward but upward: Jesus Christ loves me and gave himself for me.

The apostle Paul put it this way: "It is no longer I who live, but Christ who lives in me. And the life I now live in the flesh I live by faith in the Son of God, who loved me and gave himself for me" (Gal 2:20). Paul is saying that in the life he "now lives," he is resolved to live in the knowledge that God loves him. This is where he anchors his identity.

I trust the writers of the Heidelberg Catechism believed this too. Consider how it begins:

Q. What is your only comfort in life and in death?

A. That I am not my own, but belong—body and soul, in life and in death—to my faithful Savior, Jesus Christ. He has fully paid for all my sins with his precious blood, and has set me free from the tyranny of the devil. He also watches over me in such a way that not a hair can fall from my head without the will of my Father in heaven; in fact, all things must work together for my salvation. Because I belong to him, Christ, by his Holy Spirit, assures me of eternal life and makes me wholeheartedly willing and ready from now on to live for him.

Christians find their only firm and lasting comfort in the love God has for us.

We see this in Jesus's life. When he transitioned from carpentry to full-time, itinerant ministry, God the Father publicly shouted his delight over his Son. "This is my beloved Son, with whom I am well pleased" (Matt 3:17).

A Pillar in the Shifting Sands

I'm not great at finding my identity in Christ. During my most recent job transition, several aspects of my job changed as well. I was no longer an associate pastor but a senior teaching pastor. When this transition happened, I realized how much of my identity I tied to one particular aspect of my job: preaching. If my preaching was strong, then I was good, I was loved, and I was valuable. But if my preaching was poor, then I was bad, unloved, and valueless. In previous decades, the same issue showed up through school or sports. If I crushed an exam, then I mattered. If it crushed me, then I was crushed. Academic success became my identity.

This is antithetical to the gospel. Through God's love for us in Christ, we receive an unchanging identity, an imperishable inheritance kept in heaven for us (1 Pet 1:4). Through repentance from sin and faith in the substitutionary death and victorious resurrection of Jesus Christ, God now feels toward us the same way he feels towards his own Son: delight.

It's a long excerpt, but note how a deeper understanding of the gospel enabled author Jared Wilson to go about the job-search process:

> In 2008 I began interviewing over the phone with some people from the church I now pastor. In my former life, these calls would have racked me with anxiety. I would have been a nervous wreck. Did I say the wrong thing? Can they see through my false confidence to how inadequate I am? What if I'm not good enough? What are they saying about me when they hang up the phone? It surprised me how peaceful my spirit was throughout the interview process, and not because I always knew the answers to their questions or had an impeccable record or firsthand experience of every ministry issue raised to fall back on. I was confident because I knew who I was in Christ, and while

I wanted to make the case for their approval of me as their new pastor, I wasn't seeking their approval of me *as a person*.

This approach has practical effects. For example, I could tell in some of the lines of questioning that the search committee was placing a heavy emphasis on ministry to students. I began my ministry as a youth minister, and I was a youth minister just long enough to know that youth ministry is neither my calling nor my strength. In former days, not only would I have not said that, I would have tried to find ways to assure them of my competency and my focus on youth ministry. Because now I feel deeply the approval of God in Christ, I was able to tell them what my approach to leading a student ministry would be while also saying I have no interest in being a youth minister. Throughout the process, I felt compelled to be honest about possible quirks and complications. I'm a Calvinist. I'm an amillennialist. I drink the occasional beer. I smoke the occasional cigar. I have a "man-crush" on Tom Brady. Anything I could think of that might be an issue, I put on the table. (Okay, I didn't tell them the Tom Brady thing, but they have since figured it out and despite some nervousness haven't initiated church discipline on me yet.)[1]

If you follow Wilson on social media, you already knew about his love for the Patriots quarterback. But you can see, can't you, what a freeing difference the gospel makes in all of life, including transitions.

Dave Harvey points out something similar in his book to help Christians discern their call to pastoral ministry: "If ... my fingers have to be pried off my ministry, something went colossally wrong. That's why I need to keep my grip on the gospel. It supplies my main identity."[2]

I'm currently experiencing a season of relative stability. I don't see any transitions on the horizon, but I still strive to more deeply *re-identify* with the gospel and God's delight for me in Christ. The gospel offers green pastures and still waters, which is the only reliable remedy for the nauseating vertigo caused by a life and world in constant flux.

---

[1] Jared C. Wilson, *Gospel Wakefulness* (Wheaton: Crossway, 2011), 175–76, emphasis original.
[2] Dave Harvey, *Am I Called?: The Summons to Pastoral Ministry* (Wheaton: Crossway, 2012), 41.

Pray without Ceasing

Many people know the shortest verse in the Bible is John 11:35, "Jesus wept." However, this is only the shortest verse in English Bibles. In Greek, this verse is three words: *edakrusen o iēsous*. The shortest verse in the *original* languages is 1 Thessalonians 5:17: "Pray without ceasing." Though three words in English, it's only two words in Greek: *adialeiptōs proseuchesthe.*

Now this is just Bible trivia, but the point I want to make isn't. As Paul concludes his first letter to the church in Thessalonica, he reminds the church of the gospel: "For God has not destined [Christians] for wrath, but to obtain salvation through our Lord Jesus Christ" (5:9). After this reminder, he gives a host of short, important commands related to how Christians should live in light of the gospel. One of these commands is to "pray without ceasing."

There's good biblical precedent for prayer preceding transitions into ministry. Think of Luke 6:12, where Jesus "went out to the mountain to pray, and all night he continued in prayer to God." This was the night before "he called his disciples and chose from them twelve, whom he named apostles" (6:13). Similarly, in Acts 14:23 we read, "And when they had appointed elders for them in every church, with *prayer and fasting* they committed them to the Lord in whom they had believed."

Persistent prayer can be easy to overlook and even to neglect. There are always plenty of other things to do—writing cover letters and resumes, collecting references and recommendations, researching church websites and job boards, preparing for interviews, building a network, and so on. There's always the pressure to do "just one more thing," and prayer can easily fall by the wayside.

Don't let this happen.

As Christians, we are always *dependent* and *desperate* people— dependent on God and his grace and thus desperate for him to move on our behalf. Sometimes, like during a job search, we feel our dependence more acutely, but it's always there. Prayer acknowledges this dependence, and it's the God-appointed channel for expressing our desperate need.

When you feel overwhelmed and the job search looks anything but promising, you don't have to pray alone. Get some friends to join you. Also, don't neglect to pray with your mentors. While King Saul was hunting young David, David "fled . . . to Samuel at Ramah and told him all that Saul had done to him" (1 Sam 19:18). This short verse communicates so much. Ramah is where Samuel lived (7:17), and when things were hard—like when his boss was trying to kill him with a spear—David went back to his mentor for help.

Whoever you pray with and however you do it, just make sure you do it. If you don't depend on God when finding a job in ministry, you'll likely not rely on him once you're in ministry, which is not a pattern you want to start.

This leads to my next subject.

Trust in the Goodness and Sovereignty of God

It's imperative you keep a vibrant trust in the goodness and sovereignty of God.

Perhaps at this point you're thinking, *The goodness and sovereignty of God? Benjamin, I thought you were going to give me lots of juicy tips for finding a job in Christian ministry. Where's all the practical stuff?*

Here's the deal: there will be low moments during the job search and hiring process—very low moments. There were for me. To make it through these moments, you're must commit yourself now, before the low moments, to the truth that God is good and he is in control.

Consider what you'll do if a church you really like, maybe even the one you think could be the perfect fit, says, "We appreciate your interest but at this time we are no longer considering you for this position." *Thanks, but no thanks.* Now what are you going to do?

Or what will you do if this same church does something worse, if they say nothing at all? No calls, no e-mails, and no letters—either because they lost your resume or because they weren't considerate enough to close the loop (which is a very common experience).

Or maybe you'll realize you have to take "the list"—you know, that one you made with all the details about your *dream* job in your *dream* city with your *dream* church—and throw it in the trash. You'll have to throw it away because the job search has become so difficult and the rejections so frequent that you no longer care about finding your *dream* job—you just want *a* job.

Or maybe you'll actually get a job, even a good job, but when you move to the city, your old house doesn't sell for another eighteen months. Now all your savings are gone, and you're thinking you should sell your car. Then, to make things worse, the role you were promised at the new church doesn't turn out to be exactly what you expected or even what they expected.

These things can happen. They all happened to me.

Author and pastor Jason Helopoulos notes that candidating "usually proves to be a season of tension, nervousness, and even anxiety."[3] This shouldn't be surprising. In a sense, every job search is simply waiting for people to stop saying no.

That's an encouraging perspective, isn't it? People will keep kicking you in the shins, and when they finally stop, *then* you know you've won. This is how Quentin Schultze addresses this in his book about resumes.

> One day you'll assess yourself and your resume as outstanding. The next day you'll want to tear it up and toss it in the trash. Sometimes you'll feel like giving up. To keep your sanity, you'll want to download entire seasons of old TV shows; go shopping; hang out at a coffee shop eating pastries; or simply sleep until noon, slurp down a can of unheated SpaghettiOs, and then crawl back into bed.[4]

And yet, God has his purposes for these difficult times—even when it feels like he's trying to shake you, or even break you. As Timothy Keller writes in his book *Counterfeit Gods*, "Sometimes God seems to be killing us when he's actually saving us."[5]

---

[3] Jason Helopoulos, *The New Pastor's Handbook: Help and Encouragement for the First Years of Ministry* (Grand Rapids, MI: Baker, 2015), 32–33.

[4] Quentin J. Schultze, *Resume 101: A Student and Recent-Grad Guide to Crafting Resumes and Cover Letters that Land Jobs* (New York: Ten Speed, 2012), 8.

[5] Timothy Keller, *Counterfeit Gods: The Empty Promises of Money, Sex, and Power, and the Only Hope That Matters* (New York: Penguin, 2009), 20.

When Christians sing about the faithfulness of God, we're primarily singing about two things: God's *goodness* and God's *sovereignty*. God is *good* in that he never does evil or ultimate harm to his children. This is a wonderful thing. But if he were not also *sovereign*, then his goodness would not be much help to us because he couldn't act on it. Without sovereignty, God's goodness becomes just a platitude.

We can see our sovereign God throughout the whole narrative of the Bible. He commands nations and governs generations. From the smallest of details (such as a fish swallowing a coin) to the largest (such as the geopolitics at work in the book of Jeremiah), our God is sovereign over everything.

Scripture affirms this: "O LORD, God of our fathers . . . you rule over all the kingdoms of the nations. In your hand are power and might, so that none is able to withstand you" (2 Chr 20:6).

It's true that for some people (even some pastors), the goodness and sovereignty of God can be topics of controversy. But before these doctrines are controversial to you, I hope they are beautiful to you. After all, only a vibrant, gospel-empowered trust in the goodness and sovereignty of God will sustain you through the lows and fill you with humble gratitude during the highs.

Know Whether It's Time for a Transition

"All the time," said John Piper, "I've been thinking about it for thirty years."

What had Piper been thinking about for thirty years? Potential transition in pastoral ministry.

He said this around the time of his retirement from his long tenure at Bethlehem Baptist Church in Minnesota.[6] He continued:

> I thought about quitting a lot. Here's the beautiful thing that I look back on with such thankfulness: the Lord never let those "ready-to-move" feelings come when there was an opportunity

---

[6] Colin Hansen, "Piper on Regrets and Retirement: An Interview with Collin Hansen," *The Gospel Coalition*, April 13, 2013, https://www.thegospelcoalition.org/article/piper-on-regrets-and-retirement.

to move. The opportunities to move came when I didn't want to move. He timed it perfect.

Maybe you picked this book up "for a friend," but my guess is that you might be in one of these ready-to-move seasons right now. And yet, before we get on with the tips and tools you need to transition well, perhaps it's worth backing up to ask the question: are you sure it's the right time?

For some pastors, a looming transition is obvious. You've graduated, and you're ready to work in the field. You're being influenced by both "push" and "pull" factors, not just one or the other. You're being pushed out of seminary and pulled into a new local church. When this is the case, it's fairly straightforward. Let the transition begin.

Some of you, however, feel like you're on a rollercoaster. You feel anticipation and excitement as your church grows in size, but then a loop-de-loop and a double corkscrew induces fear and instability. How do you know when your time is done? If you were terminated, others decided the ride for you was over. But what about when the decision is yours?

Determining God's will is often tricky. Gideon used a fleece, but I'm not sure this was to his credit. So we probably shouldn't try something similar.

When I was a kid, my parents gave me a choice about a summer vacation. I couldn't figure out what to do. My parents told me I could go with them on a short trip to visit my grandparents or I could stay home with a friend to attend a local basketball camp. I had no idea what God wanted me to do. One morning I distinctly remember staring at a small bowl of cereal and asking God this very question. As I twirled the last few Lucky Charms with my spoon, I asked God to make the cereal into the shape of the state—either Missouri (basketball) or Iowa (grandparents)—to indicate what I should do. I'm not encouraging you to go and do likewise. After all, when I was a child . . .

Kevin DeYoung writes these words on how to discern the will of God:

"The will of God" is one of the most confusing phrases in the Christian vocabulary. Sometimes we speak of all things happening according to God's will. Other times we talk about being obedient and doing the will of God. And still other times we talk about finding the will of God.[7]

Too often we feel as though we need to divine God's will (say, with Lucky Charms). But DeYoung argues we should stop "thinking of God's will like a corn maze, or a tightrope, or a bull's-eye."[8] Instead, we need to realize God gave us brains and passions and mentors and friends and education and experiences and longings. As we listen to all of these—as well as when we adequately take into account our proclivity for sinful, mixed motives—somehow God shows himself faithful to lead us to where we should go.

In his book *Before You Move*, John Cionca explains thirty-five different categories to help pastors sense whether God is moving them to another ministry. He uses the metaphor of red and green traffic lights. The more red lights, the less likely God may be moving you, and the more green lights, the more likely he may be. So, if you get nineteen green lights and sixteen red lights, that makes things clearer, right? No, it's not a simple math problem, and neither do each of the thirty-five categories carry equal weight.

But I do find it helpful how this approach forces one to think broadly about the situation. Often when a pastor wants to move, it might be that a few persistent annoyances have provoked his restless desire. It's better to consider the whole picture.

I won't list all of his thirty-five categories, but here are some I found especially useful.

Red Lights to Moving	**Green Lights to Moving**
Congregational Hunger	Congregational Apathy
Vibrancy and Growth	Stagnation and Decline
Good Giftedness Match	Poor Giftedness Match
Enthusiasm for the Task	Restlessness or Withdrawal
Good Opportunity for Impact	Limited Opportunity for Impact

---

[7] Kevin DeYoung, *Just Do Something: A Liberating Approach to Finding God's Will* (Chicago: Moody, 2009), 16.
[8] Ibid., 23.

Family Happy and Growing	Family Distressed and Stifled
Appropriate Compensation	Insufficient Compensation
Tenure Less than Six Years	Tenure More than Six Years
Compatibility with Staff	Poor Staff or Key Relationships
High Integrity and Credibility	Low Integrity and Credibility
Advisors Confirm Ministry	Advisors Suggest Major Change
Ideal Geographical Proximity to Extended Family	Less than Ideal Geographical Proximity to Extended Family

Again, these don't provide a full-proof plan; they're simply tools. If the prophets Isaiah and Jeremiah had used these categories, the score would have been a shutout: 0–35. They were certainly in one of those ready-to-move seasons. Often, a prophet's congregation didn't want to fire him but to kill him. In fact, when God explains to Isaiah that his job description involved preaching until the pews were not only empty but until they were burned to ashes, Isaiah's "Here am I! Send me" quickly became "How long, O Lord?" For Isaiah (and many other prophets), faithfulness meant staying put when all the lights appeared to be green. Why? Because the voice of God became to them like Gandalf thrusting down his staff and roaring, "You shall not pass!"

If, however, God is telling you it might be time for a transition, then keep reading so we can talk about how to find the right job with excellence, integrity, and respect for everyone involved.

* * *

"Is God Calling Me to Be a Pastor?"

By David Mathis

It's a question many Christians wrestle with at some point in their life of faith. Not just in adolescence or early adulthood, but sometimes midlife, or even in approaching so-called retirement age. Maybe that's why you picked up Benjamin's book. If so, there are three questions you should be asking.

Do I desire the work? (Aspiration) God wants pastors to want to do the work. He wants elders who happily give of themselves in this emotionally taxing work, "not reluctantly or under compulsion" (2 Cor 9:7). God loves a cheerful pastor.

When the apostle Paul addresses the qualifications of pastors-elders-overseers, he first mentions aspiration. "The saying is trustworthy: If anyone *aspires* to the office of overseer, he desires a noble task" (1 Tim 3:1). God wants men who want to do the work, not men who do it simply out of a sense of duty. He grabs pastors by the heart; he doesn't twist them by the arm.

Peter may say it most powerfully. Christ wants elders to shepherd (pastor) his flock "not under compulsion, but willingly, *as God would have you*" (1 Pet 5:2). How remarkable that pastoring from aspiration and delight, not obligation and duty, would be "as God would have you." This is the kind of God we have—the desiring (not dutiful) God, who wants pastors who are desiring (not dutiful) pastors. Such a happy God means for the leaders of his church to do their work "with joy and not with groaning, for that would be of no advantage" to the people (Heb 13:17).

Has God gifted me for it? (Affirmation) After sensing a subjective desire for pastoral ministry, we need to ask a more objective question about our gifting. Have I seen evidence, however small, of fruitfulness in serving others through biblical teaching and counsel? And, even more important than my own self-assessment, do others confirm my giftings for pastoral ministry?

This is the opposite of the "follow your heart" perspective and "don't settle for anything less than your dreams" ideology we so often hear in society. What's most important in discerning God's call is not bringing the desires of our heart to bear on the world, but letting the needs of others shape our heart.

Before you go looking for opportunities to shepherd in the future, make sure you are able to meet real spiritual needs in front of you today and seek confirmation from your current local church and Christian community.

Has he opened the door? (Opportunity) Perhaps most often overlooked in Christian discussions of calling is the actual God-given, real-world open door. You may *feel* called, and others may *affirm* your general direction, but you are not yet fully "called" to a specific pastoral ministry until God opens the door.

In my experience, we often leave out this final reality-check step. We say that a seminary student who aspires to preach and has received affirmation from his home church is "called to ministry." Well, not yet. He aspires to full-time ministry, thank God, and some people have found his giftings helpful. He is well on his way. But what this aspiring, affirmed brother doesn't yet have is a real-live opportunity where some ministry or church presents a job description and says, "We are ready to call you to pastor here. Would you accept?"

Until God, through a specific local church, *makes* a man an overseer (Acts 20:28), *gives* him to the church (Eph 4:11–12), *sends* him as a laborer (Matt 9:37–38; Rom 10:14–15), and *sets* him over his household (Luke 12:42), he is not yet fully called.

But what a marvel and blessing it is when God gives a man a desire for the pastoral office, gifts him to meet real needs in the church with the word of God and wisdom, with affirmation from a specific local body of Christ, and opens a door for him to lead and serve in a specific local church. Then he knows he is called.

David Mathis is executive editor for desiringGod.org and pastor at Cities Church in Minneapolis. He is a husband, father of four, and author of *Habits of Grace: Enjoying Jesus through the Spiritual Disciplines.*

PART ONE

SMOKING *The* CURVE

DON'T *Just* SEND A RESUME

WRITE CUSTOM COVER LETTERS AND RESUMES

I, Paul, write this greeting with my own hand. This is the sign of genuineness in every letter of mine; it is the way I write.
– 2 Thessalonians 3:17

The 200-meter race is a sprint—only half a lap around the track. It takes the best men in the world just under twenty seconds and the rest of us somewhere in the twenties. You start the race on the curve and finish on the straightaway.

My high school sprint coach, Coach Grosso, was a short and intense Italian. He could bench press all the weights in the gym, and he perennially wore a tank top, even in winter (at least inside). I remember many of the things Coach Grosso taught us but especially how to run the 200-meter race.

So, what was his secret? He'd pull us in close and in his raspy, passionate voice, he'd say, "Boys, if you want to run a fast 200, ya gotta smoke the curve."

"Smoke the curve" is track-speak for starting fast. You need to get out of the blocks clean; don't hold anything back. Because if you hold back at the start, it won't matter how fast you can finish.

I don't know if this remains the best coaching advice for running the 200-meter or not. I wasn't very good at the race, but that's because I was slow, not because I was poorly coached. Regardless, if you want to find a job in Christian ministry, ya gotta smoke the curve. When the gun goes off, you need to be ready to run. If you don't start strong, you won't get a chance to end strong because the process will already be over.

When I was looking for my first pastoral job, I thought I knew how important the initial contact would be. However, I wasn't ready for what I experienced. After I'd sent my cover letter and resume to one church, I called to see how the process was going and to let them know I was interested. The kind woman who answered the phone said, "It's so nice of you to call. The search is going great." When I asked how many people had applied, she said, "I think it's up to three hundred." A few weeks later I applied to another church, and in that search I later found out I was one of six hundred candidates from eleven different countries!

See what I mean? If you don't start strong, a church may be moving on without you, even if you're an excellent candidate.

I'm now several years removed from these experiences and can say that the size of those searches is on the high end, but they're not unheard of, especially for a large church that posts a well-crafted job description on a major website.

Always Include a Short, Custom Cover Letter

It's common to hear people talk of sending their resume to an employer. Never do this. Or I should say, never *just* send a resume.

Why? Because the cover letter, not the resume, is the leading edge of your job search. Merely sending a resume (at least in ministry) accomplishes little more than spamming a search committee. It's lazy and rarely stands out from the stack. Sending a custom cover letter, however, shows you care. And pastors should care.

Many job search guides in the business world will tell you the primary focus is on the resume. I've been told that for many huge companies (think: Procter & Gamble and IBM), resumes are usually read before cover letters. Additionally, a resume might remain in large resume "banks" for recall. In these situations, some of the standard advice about resumes (like including key word optimization for enhanced searchability) makes sense.

But in ministry, things are different. The vast majority of churches will open a hiring process, complete a hiring process, and then throw everything away or save it for a year, then throw it away. This makes the process far more personal. Furthermore, churches don't have a full-time HR person who spends his or her day scanning resumes. So when a church conducts a search, it will likely read or at least skim your cover letter first. So make it count.

Having said that, much of your cover letter can be boilerplate, meaning you can use most (but not all) of the verbiage with little to no modification. It should include the following descriptions:

- this (briefly) is who I am;
- this (briefly) is where I worked;
- this is where I went to school;
- this is where you can listen to my sermons (or watch videos of me leading worship);
- this is what I'm passionate about and why you should hire me.

I won't tell you exactly what to write, but stuff like this is expected and appropriate.

More than anything else, don't make it generic. If everything in your cover letter could be sent to every church in America, then your cover letter will be underwhelming and most likely overlooked. Like a good sermon, letters have a particular audience in mind. Therefore, tailor at least one paragraph to demonstrate the following three things to the church.

First, demonstrate you actually read the job description. No job is exactly the same, even if they both share the title "youth pastor." Someone, or likely several people, spent significant time wording the job description, and it will serve you well to show them you cared enough to read it closely.

Second, demonstrate why you think you would be a good fit at this particular church and location. To do this, make sure you spend time on the church's website. Perhaps in this paragraph you can even comment on something you see on their church calendar or some connection you have to their city or state (if you have one).

Let's say the church is in a town called Springfield. You might say something like, "I've lived in Springfield all my life" or "When I was a child, we took a vacation and stayed near Springfield. Such a beautiful area." If you see the church is hosting Financial Peace University by Dave Ramsey, and you've led that before, let them know. If last fall they preached a series called "The Gospel According to Genesis," tell them you've preached through the book as well and you love their series title. But don't get too wordy. Cover letters should be short, never more than one page single spaced.

Third, make sure you address your letter to an actual person or at a minimum "Search Team for 'Such-and-Such' Church." Don't use "To Whom It May Concern." It's out of date and smacks (again) of spam.

I have just one more thing to say: accuracy! This applies to everything you send to a church but especially to the leading edge. Have your cover letter edited several times by others who can snipe a typo from 1,000 yards away. If you get to the place where you're frequently e-mailing with a church, then don't slow the process down by getting someone to edit your e-mails. But short of this, aim for grammatical perfection.

If you don't have the time or money for professional editing, and you don't trust the ability of your friends, there are several things you can do to improve the quality of your self-editing. First, run the spell check. Simple, right? Yet it's often not done. Make sure to do it even if you think you're golden. Second, print what you wrote and read it aloud. Most people catch more typos when they're *not* reading silently from a screen. Third, use editing software on the Internet. My two favorites are the Hemingway App and Grammarly.[1] Fourth, if you have time, put the document away for a few days. It can be difficult to see your own mistakes when you're too close to them. I think this is something of a spiritual metaphor. Finally, use software that can "read" out

---

[1] www.hemingwayapp.com and www.grammarly.com. Both are available in free and paid versions. Also, Grammarly has an add-on for Chrome and Outlook to help with e-mails.

loud so your document can be read back to you. My favorite is Natu-ralReader.[2] Electronic readers all sound a little choppy and mechanical, but you're not listening for eloquence; you're listening for typos. This final layer of self-editing is where I often catch mistakes I never would have found otherwise. If you don't want to mess with finding software to do this, many smartphones are able to read text. A quick Internet search will show you how to do this.

Choose the Right Resume Style for You

Now let's talk about resumes. I mentioned that when you're searching for a job in ministry, you should never just send a resume. Another misconception is that your resume is the key to getting you a job. A resume (and cover letter, references, and recommendation letter) don't get you the job; they get you interviews. Interviews get you the job. In chapter 6 we'll spend lots of time talking about interviews. For now, let's keep talking about the details that get you those interviews. I'll start with the main decision you'll have to make about your resume and then move on to some of the minor and more subjective aspects.

When drafting a resume, the first choice you must make is organizational structure. There are two basic approaches to structure: (1) the traditional, business style and (2) the skill-based style.

In the **traditional style**, you state, "I worked *here* and did *X, Y, and Z; before that,* I worked *here* and did *X, Y, and Z.*" The traditional style is chronological. You begin with your most recent experience and then move into the past. This allows readers to scan your work experience and education quickly. Because this is most prevalent in the business sphere, it will likely appeal most to those on the search team who work in business.

The other approach is a **skill-based** resume. This highlights three or four skills that are particularly suited to ministry (say preaching, administration, leading short-term missions) and then explains when and where you've developed and used them. I've no statistics on this, but in my experience people who work in a church tend to like this

---

² www.naturalreaders.com. As with the Hemingway App and Grammarly, you can use Natu-ralReader on the Internet or download it for your desktop.

style; it helps us to quickly see your strengths. Additionally, the skill-based resume helps a candidate highlight skills even if he's had minimal ministry experience or has developed his skills in non-ministry jobs.

If you have time, you might even try both styles and do some informal market research by showing them to other pastors and business leaders. "Hey, could you look at these and tell me which one is better?" Internet marketers call this A/B testing.

Once you decide on structure, there are several other aspects you'll want to consider. Admittedly, these are subjective decisions. There's no agreed-upon format that *all* people in *all* situations should follow; there are only best practices.

Contact Information

Make sure you include your name and contact information at the top: address, phone, e-mail, social media,[3] and website if you have one. Include this information even if it feels redundant. You'd hate to have a church excited about you but not sure how to reach you.

If you anticipate moving soon, put a note after the address like "until May 15, 2019." You might even list a "current address" and a "permanent address." This is most common and acceptable when people are graduating from college or seminary.

How you lay out this information is a matter of personal preference. Two lines or three? Centered text? Bold text? I'll say more about aesthetic choices later, but for now I'll just say this: make it professional and simple. No frills is best.

How Much Detail?

If you're coming straight out of seminary, don't worry too much about how this looks on paper because there's not much you can do about it. Just include what church experience you do have, even if it's part-time or volunteer. Your non-ministry work experience is also helpful. This is especially true if you went straight through Christian grade school,

---

[3] For those interested in a youth ministry position, know that churches will most certainly be checking for these.

Christian high school, Bible college, and seminary. Seeing that you worked at the post office or in a candy factory helps a church know you don't smell like a library and sound like a Hallmark movie. Also, when you list experience, the assumption is you are noting full-time work. If it was part-time or volunteer work, flag it as such.

Churches don't need exhaustive details about each job. They don't need to know your job required you to send e-mails. If, however, you've officiated weddings and funerals, that's nice to know. If you've done pulpit supply, include this too. Other things that might be included are military service; special awards; community and civic involvement; written material, especially things published; the ability to speak a foreign language; recorded music albums; areas in which you volunteer; and continuing education.

As you add information, whether under experience or education, use symmetrical wording and consistent formatting. The bullet-points should all start with an action verb and end without a period. Also, communicate accomplishments, not just responsibilities. Don't say, "Oversaw the small group ministry," but rather something like, "Strengthened and grew the small group ministry from 13 to 39 groups." On my resume for a pastoral internship, for example, I included the following three bullet points:

- Preached three expository sermons congruent with the church's series through Genesis
- Experienced a variety of ministries (worked with youth and adult small groups; visited members; and attended elder and new-building committee meetings)
- Led three-week study to 50+ adults and youth through curriculum I authored called *A Short Study of The Bible, Homosexuality & Culture: Helping Christians Navigate the Issues* (available upon request)

Looking at these today, they seem too wordy, as if I was trying too hard. They don't really communicate accomplishments either. But you get the point.

Finally, unless you've been at it for a long time, shoot for making your resume one page.

Ministry Objective

It's common to place a statement near the top of the resume that indicates your broad intentions for employment. It usually goes something like this:

> Ministry Objective: To work as an associate teaching pastor in a mid-sized church.

Although common, this objective is unnecessary because your custom cover letter should state your objective.

Look at it like this. In a cover letter you might write this sentence: "I would love to work for Community PCA as the pastor over Christian Education. I would connect well with your congregation while also reaching the university students and young professionals who live near your church." If, however, you wrote the equivalent of these two sentences as an objective on your resume, it would be far too specific.

> Ministry Objective: To work in a PCA church near a local university as the pastor of Christian Education.

This job probably exists, but again, it's far too specific. Consider also that the other end of the spectrum is too broad. Saying you want to "work for a church" helps no one because it's too general. So I encourage you to omit the objective.

Some suggest that your resume should include your "philosophy of ministry." This probably doesn't fit unless it's very, very brief (i.e., "Love God; love people"). It's usually best to leave it off. You don't want to exclude yourself from a place where you might actually love to work (and they might love to have you).

These same sentiments apply to mission/vision statements and doctrinal statements. You can send these later if they're requested.

Grade Point Average

Most people list their work experience first and put their education underneath. This is what I prefer. If you're coming straight out of seminary and have an exceptional GPA and are graduating *cum laude* or *magna cum laude* or *summa cum something*, you can include it. If not, leave it blank. Churches don't care about GPAs, and if they do, let them ask.

References

As for references, you'll see more comments in the next chapter, but now I'll tell you to include them. At the bottom of your resume, however, *do not* put "References: Available upon request," but rather "References: See attached."

Customization and Integrity

Finally, as with your cover letter, I would encourage you to tailor the verbiage of your resume to the specific job description. One expert notes, any person "could have six or eight different resumes, all of them honest representations of past experience."[4] Another expert writes, "Fine-tune each resume as well as each cover letter. Think in terms of what the organization wants to read, not in terms of what you want to write. . . . Don't, under any circumstances, *submit a generic resume.*"[5]

But don't misunderstand: you shouldn't just tell a church what you think it wants to hear. Deceit of any kind will—and should—disqualify you immediately. But you can legitimately fit a square peg through an octagon-shaped hole if you turn it the right way. So, if the prospective job requires it, emphasize your experience leading contemporary music or working with junior high students or preaching regularly or launching small groups.

Now that you have your resume and cover letter together, let's talk about other things you should have ready to send to a church.

---

[4] Orville Pierson, *The Unwritten Rules of the Highly Effective Job Search: The Proven Program Used by the World's Leading Career Services Company* (New York: McGraw-Hill, 2006), 18.
[5] Schultze, *Resume 101*, 43, 61, emphasis original.

*   *   *

"Early Discernment at the Beginning of God's Call"

By Sam Rainer

When I started pastoring, I had little doubt I would remain a bi-vocational pastor indefinitely. I enjoyed my corporate job. I clearly understood my calling to pastor. In what I thought was an ideal arrangement, I served my church in the evenings and on the weekends while maintaining my day job. But after two years God called me to serve another church full-time. The season of ministry changed. My income went down, and my stress went up. But—for the most part—I remained content.

A certain (uncomfortable) peace comes with following God's call.

Recently I started a group in my church dubbed "Project Shepherd." The goal of the group is to equip men called to lead the church—future preachers, pastors, and missionaries. When I floated the idea to my church, little did I know two dozen men would step forward and acknowledge God had called them. The group is four times the size of my first church.

Hearing them verbalize their callings brought back emotions from the beginning of my calling. I was certain God had called me to pastor. I was not certain exactly what that meant. The guys in my Project Shepherd group know they're called, and I'm going to enjoy watching God gradually reveal who he will send where. The common theme with this group is the question, "How do I know what I'm supposed to do?" Obviously, the church confirms and affirms an individual in a specific calling. But how do you get to the specifics of your general calling?

I shared with my group three filters for early discernment: position, church, and place. These three frames can help narrow a calling.

Position. Some church leaders are called to a specific position. For instance, you may know college ministry is where God is leading you. It doesn't matter where you serve geographically. It doesn't matter in what church or ministry you serve. All that matters is serving college students. If you're called to a specific position, then you can be more open to serving in a variety of geographic settings and churches.

Church. Some are called to a specific church. The position does not matter as much as serving a particular local congregation. Those called to serve a specific church have the freedom to volunteer and the flexibility to serve in a variety of positions.

Place. Some are called to a specific place. Whether it is a cross-cultural setting or a region, state, or city in the United States, those with this calling are drawn to a place. Those called to a particular place may not even have a clear understanding of the ministry or position, but they know clearly where they are to serve.

As you work through a calling, God lifts the veil of uncertainty and begins to refine the call. Praying through a position, church, or place, however, can help with early discernment in this process.

Sam Rainer serves as lead pastor of West Bradenton Baptist Church in Bradenton, Florida. He is the president of Rainer Research, the co-founder/co-owner of Rainer Publishing, the author of *Obstacles in the Established Church*, coauthor of *Essential Church*, and the cohost of the *Established Church* podcast.

CORRESPOND LIKE A PROFESSIONAL

Moreover, he must be well thought of by outsiders.
– 1 Timothy 3:7

I've been to enough restaurants and watched enough cooking shows to know a meal's presentation is almost as important as how it tastes. If your fork and knife still have steak juice from the previous meal on them, and if your food is tossed on the plate like they are throwing slop to pigs, it won't matter if Gordon Ramsay cooked the food. The same goes for what you send to churches. In this chapter we'll learn some suggestions on how to combine good food with good presentation.

As we covered in chapter 1, the information you send to a church will primarily include a cover letter and resume. But there are several other things you might also send throughout the process. In this chapter we'll talk about sermon samples, references, and recommendation letters. I'll also make some comments about how to package this information.

With Sermon Audio and Video Samples, Suggest a Few of the Best but Give Them Several

In some church traditions, what we now typically call a "pastoral search team (or committee)" had previously been called a pulpit committee.[1] But regardless of what the church calls it, if the job description involves any amount of preaching, they'll want to hear samples.

Early in the process, pick your best two sermons and tell the search team where they can listen to them online. If you're fortunate enough to have your sermons available on video, take your favorite message, create a two-minute clip of it, and then post it somewhere online like Vimeo (avoid YouTube, which tends to be cluttered with ads, some of them lewd).

Because churches often receive more inquiries than they can manage, a solid two-minute clip is sometimes all a church needs at the start. You can always send more later. A pastor at a large church once told me he wouldn't even consider a candidate until he's seen a video of the individual. But keep this in mind: if the only video footage you have is lame in terms of production quality, don't show it to people. Footage of you preaching in a seminary classroom—if it's anything like mine—definitely falls in this category. In this case, only give audio links.

Speaking of audio, only give your best sermon or two while you're in the early stages of the hiring process. Later, encourage the search team to listen to at least a dozen of your sermons that you *don't* hand-pick. For their sake—and yours—a diet of your typical preaching should be sampled. Sure, we all have one great sermon. But such sermons aren't reflective of our norm, and hiring expectations must be grounded in the typical, not the exceptional. Again, this is for your sake *and* theirs. Chris Brauns, writing to pastoral search teams, suggests something similar:

---

[1] Robert L. Sheffield, *Pastor Search Committee Handbook, Revised* (Nashville, TN: LifeWay, 2002), 8.

You might say to the candidate, "Please send us the last four sermons you preached." But you might be wise to add this request: "Please also send us a couple sermons of your own choosing." It might be nice to know what he thinks is one of his better efforts.[2]

This advice is straightforward if you've been preaching for several years, but you might be asking, "What if I don't have sermon audio?" Good question. This is common for seminary grads, but there are easy ways to work around it. When you do preach (in your own church or as a guest in other churches) make sure you get a recording. If you preach at a church that doesn't record, as I did for a few months in seminary, you'll have to do it on your own. You can use your iPhone, or if you want to improve the quality without spending much money, I'd suggest an entry-level handheld digital recorder coupled with a lapel microphone.[3]

If you're a worship leader, this applies to you as well. But at some point you'll likely have to find a way to show video. So if you don't have this already, get it. Even if it means recruiting some friends with the necessary skills and equipment and "leading worship" when no one is in the sanctuary.

Later in the book I'll say more about *when* and *whom* to tell about a transition. For now, suffice it to say that you should tell your senior leadership early. I'm bringing this up now because when you're preparing some of the first documents you'll send to churches, you don't want your pastor walking into the sanctuary after youth group only to ask why you're making a music video. Awkward.

Include High-quality Pictures and a Family Bio

In your correspondence include pictures of yourself and, if you're married, pictures of your family. In the business world you generally don't do this. It's often not even allowed. But ministry is different. It's about relationships and knowing one another.

---

[2] Chris Brauns, *When the Word Leads Your Pastoral Search Pastoral Search: Biblical Principles & Practices to Guide Your Search* (Chicago: Moody, 2011), 126.
[3] The Samson Zoom H1 is a good entry-level recorder and costs only $100.

Perhaps you're asking, "Where do I put these pictures? In the e-mail? On the cover letter?" Again, good questions. Here's what you do. Write a short biographical sketch of your family and put the picture at the top of the page. The writing should be informal and conversational. This is another chance to display your writing and people skills. In the book *From M.Div. to Rev*, Eubanks suggests including things such as where you grew up, distinctive aspects of college, your hobbies, where you worked before seminary, and any particularly life-shaping experiences. If you're married, you might share how you met your spouse.[4]

Here's what I wrote for a bio seven years ago. I share it not as a model of perfection but as an example to stir your creative juices.

> We took this picture [which I had placed above] in front of our house a few weeks ago. The tree behind us has more than doubled in size since we moved into our house five years ago. So has our family.
>
> My oldest daughter, Noah (4), loves "accessorizing," and if given the chance, she would wear every belt, bracelet, and barrette that she owns. Hudson (2.5) is "all boy," as they say. When we act out the David and Goliath story, he wants to be *both* David and Goliath so he can hold Goliath's sword and David's slingshot. Eden was born this summer. She is the best sleeper of the lot, for which we are deeply thankful! My wife, Brooke, and I are in our sixth year of marriage. We met through a Bible study in the athletic department at the University of Missouri. We both competed on the track & field team; she was much better than I was. In fact, Brooke was even recently inducted into her high school's athletic hall of fame, so I like to joke that I have a hall of fame wife.
>
> The last few years have been anything but easy, yet God has been exceedingly good to us and we are eager to begin ministry in a more focused way among the people of God in a local congregation.

---

[4] J. E. Eubanks Jr., *From M.Div. to Rev.: Making an Effective Transition from Seminary into Pastoral Ministry* (Oakland, TN: Doulos Resources, 2011), 110–11.

Don't create a carbon copy of my bio. Just be yourself. A pastor's bio should be like sharing a cup of coffee with a new friend.

Select Quality and Diverse References

It's common for candidates to have references "available upon request." I understand why people do this; either they don't want to overwhelm churches with lots of paper or they want to wait until the job search has progressed before they gather this info. Perhaps this is because the transition may be a secret for the time. I'd discourage this approach. Provide references right away. It shows you have nothing to hide, and if you're serious about the job, you'll have to provide them at some point anyway.

I suggest picking a diverse group of references. For example, you might choose a seminary professor, a former pastor, someone in your congregation who works in business, and the parent of a child in your youth group. Try to include both men and women, and if you're brave, I'd encourage you to include a reference from a non-Christian. Remember, it's a requirement for pastors to "be well thought of by outsiders" (1 Tim 3:7).

Let me spend just a moment talking about what it means to be well thought of by outsiders. A more literal rendering of this verse would be something like, "it is necessary also to have a good testimony from outsiders."[5] Notice that outsiders (*tōn exōthen*) is plural. The good testimony is singular, but those who witness to it are many. Also consider how the language of testimony calls to mind the image of a courtroom. In other words, if a judge called a prospective pastor before a jury and he was not allowed to have Christians to testify on his behalf, would even unbelievers be able to testify in his favor? Paul wants Timothy to appoint elders who can find people to vouch for their character.

In the context of 1 Timothy 3:1–7, it's clear God wants pastors to have a well-rounded character that's tested in all spheres of life: the church, the family, and the world. All Christians, but especially

---

[5] Author's translation.

ministry leaders, must not compartmentalize their lives but rather be able to engage graciously with people of all backgrounds.

Now let's get back to your references. In addition to their contact information, make sure to include a short description of your relationship to each person. You might say something like, "Anthony has been my neighbor for the last ten years. He's not a Christian, but we're good friends and have had many conversations about the gospel." Or, "Steve is the worship pastor at our church. We work closely together, and our families are dear friends."

While I was in seminary, I worked for a construction company where I knew many non-believers who became close friends. In fact, one of my references was from a co-worker named Matthew. Next to his name on the paperwork I gave to churches, I wrote,

> Matt has been my co-worker and boss for the last five years at the construction company I work for in Saint Louis. His father is the owner of the company. Matt is an active member of his Mormon church (LDS), which has led to some good dialogue between us.

Here's a final point about references. As the search process moves forward, it's appropriate to give your references a heads-up that they may be getting a call soon. You don't want them to be surprised. A surprised reference is usually not a good reference. It's your job to keep them up to speed.

Some will list people as references without asking them first. That's a bad idea. If their name and contact information is on the page, assume they can be called at any time. A well-meaning search team can easily miss your note. Then what will you do?

One of my associate pastor friends recalled this story to me: "One night after a leader meeting, [my senior pastor and boss] asked me to stay after to talk. I thought he just wanted to debrief something from the meeting. And he looked at me and said, 'Is there anything you'd like me to tell the church you're interviewing with when I call them back tomorrow?'" In the providence of God, my friend said, this potentially terrible situation improved the health of their relationship as it led them into greater openness about the future. But this certainly won't always be the case.

Consider Sending a Recommendation Letter

My wife and I read books differently. She's been known to skip a preface or two and maybe even a few other pages along the way. I, on the other hand, won't ever skip a page. I'm peculiar like that.

There is, however, even for me, an exception to this rule. I *never* read the pages at the very front of a book titled "In praise of _____." If you ask me, these pages aren't even meant to be read, at least not closely. They're just there to help sell the book and bolster its credibility.

A recommendation letter is sort of like that. It's nice to have because, at a glance, it legitimizes a candidate. But that's about all. If you decide to send one, here are a few ways to make the most of it. First, realize a recommendation letter doesn't have to be from a Christian celebrity for it to be helpful. If John Piper or Beth Moore or Rick Warren wants to write you a recommendation letter, then sweet. But don't worry if they aren't available. The other people applying for the job don't have one from these people either.

It'll be *more* helpful if you get a letter from a former supervisor or someone you oversaw (such as a youth leader). The most effective letter, however, would be from someone who's already known by and has the respect of the church at which you are applying. Recently, we hired a full-time youth and music director. He didn't send us a recommendation letter, but he did have on his references two men we already knew and respected. He listed these men as references, but each of them would have been excellent candidates for recommendation letters.

Second, if you don't know someone familiar to the church, then find someone interesting to write the recommendation. When I was transitioning from engineering to pastoring, I asked one of my former pastors to write a recommendation letter. I also asked my Muslim engineering co-worker.

Obviously, my Muslim co-worker couldn't speak to my preaching ability or how well I could lead a small group. But because we'd worked closely together for several years, he was able to comment on my character and teamwork and even how we'd engaged each other in conversations about religion. Churches seemed to find his letter helpful.

Finally, don't lead with your recommendation letter. When you send your information to a church, I recommend this order:

1) *cover letter*
2) *resume*
3) *pastor-family bio*
4) *references*
5) *recommendation letter(s)*

Use Simple, Professional Formatting

If you want to be taken seriously, simple and professional formatting is essential. I can't tell you how many times I've looked at resumes with goofy margins or fonts. Also, make sure to keep all the fonts consistent. It matters.

Whatever you decide, don't get cute. Choose a simple, standard font, or at most, tactfully and consistently blend two of them. If you opt to use a bunch of weird, artsy fonts, you'll stand out but probably not in the right way.

Only Send PDFs (Not Microsoft Word Documents)

Never send your information in Microsoft Word documents. You can't control how a Word document will look on another person's computer screen. You can, however, control how a PDF looks. PDF stands for "portable document format." They exist for exactly this reason.

When I've been on search committees, every time I've looked at a printed resume with scrambled formatting, it has proved a major distraction. A PDF eliminates this possibility. Send a PDF to protect your hard work.

If you do not know how to save a document as a PDF, Google it or ask someone for help. Don't be lazy with this. It's important.

Send Only One Attachment

If you've paid attention so far, then you know you'll be sending several documents: a cover letter, a resume, a bio with picture(s), references, and possibly a recommendation letter. However, do *not* send an e-mail with a bunch of attachments. Multiple attachments are annoying and impractical. There's a chance the person receiving the e-mail could accidentally not print one of them. As I said above, your one attachment should be a PDF.

You might be asking, "But what if each of the documents is in a different Word document—how do I make them into one PDF?" This isn't a problem. Save each as a PDF and then merge them into one PDF document. If you don't own a program that can do this, you can Google "merge PDF" and you'll see several options.[6]

Send Communication from Your Personal E-mail Account

Under no circumstances should you send this information through the mechanism provided by some job-search websites or your denomination's forum. This might feel like the easy button, but don't press it.

Instead, if you find a job listing on a common job-search website, try to find the individual church's website to see if the church has posted the opening there as well. If so, there will often be supplementary information available, specifically about whom to e-mail. Job posting banks typically have stock input forms, and going straight to the source lets you see how the church desires to present themselves.

Related to sending your information to a church, don't have a cheesy e-mail address. You know what I mean. Don't have an e-mail address like,

IAmSoOnFireForJesus@aol.com, or
18sg32@yahoo.com

---

[6] My favorite is www.pdfmerge.com.

The first e-mail address is both cheesy and dated, and the second is cryptic and non-specific. Additionally, don't use your student or current work e-mail. This is true for multiple reasons but mainly because people might try to contact you after you have left your current school or employer but won't be able to. You want an e-mail that will stay with you after you leave. If you don't have an e-mail like this, just create one at Gmail containing your first and last name.

When you e-mail your information, resist the urge to cut and paste your cover letter into the body of the e-mail. Instead, write a short, informal e-mail that shares (1) who you are, (2) your interest in the opening, (3) that you attached more information, and (4) that you'd like a brief response to confirm it was received. Your e-mail might look something like this:

Re: Applying for the Associate Pastor Opening

Hello! I saw your job opening on ChurchStaffing.com and your church website. It looks like you have a wonderful church.

I'm a graduating seminary student from _____ with several years of pastoral experience. I'd love to talk more about this opening. I've attached the requested information to this e-mail.

Looking forward to hearing from you,
Benjamin

P.S. Could you please shoot me a quick e-mail to let me know this e-mail was received? Thanks![7]

I don't think this approach is too informal, though I know it's out of step with the standard advice in job-search books. In the business world, it would be appropriate that the body of your e-mail be identical to your cover letter, if not in place of the cover letter altogether. However, this is another place where the differences between formal

---

[7] I've heard many, many pastors say that even though they've included a similar postscript, they didn't hear anything back, not even an automated reply e-mail. Still, follow up at least once even if this is the case.

ministry and businesses mean that you, as the candidate, need to modify your methods.

Most churches don't hire people frequently. Even a healthy, growing church, if it's under 2,000 people (the threshold for the epithet "mega"), won't typically hire someone more than once a year. This means that when a church posts an opening, they want people to respond, and they'll be reading what's sent to them. It's also why you need to think through what you send to make sure that you're both confident and thoughtful.

*   *   *

"Let the Word Lead Your Church Search"

By Chris Brauns

Given the centrality of the local church in God's plan for this age, few topics are more important than helping local churches call the right pastoral candidates. For that reason, I wrote my book, *When the Word Leads Your Pastoral Search*. Likewise, I heartily recommend *Don't Just Send a Resume*, and I am humbled by the opportunity to give a brief word of encouragement.

My advice for pastoral candidates is the same that I give to local churches: *let the Word lead your search!* In offering the counsel to allow God's Word to lead the search for a pastoral position, I am not suggesting that only those factors immediately and obviously connected to a particular verse of Scripture should be considered. As Benjamin describes in this book, dozens of factors should be considered. At least the 131 questions he provides in this book should be asked!

But in the often-foggy days of stalking churches on the Internet and sifting through information about demographics or the cost of housing in a particular area, it is of vital importance that you discipline yourself to look down at the compass of God's Word with every step you take forward. Keep re-orienting yourself by meditating on the Word.

If you're like me, you might respond to this challenge of letting the Word lead your search by asking for practical suggestions. What are specific strategies that can be implemented to allow the Word to be the compass in a pastoral search? One very practical way to go about making sure your search is led by the Word is to *memorize* a passage like 1 Timothy 3:14–4:16. Doing so would serve your search in many different ways.

1. Paul's purpose statement for the letter in 1 Timothy 3:14–16 offers an ideal beginning point for speaking Christocentrically with search committees about the purpose of the local church and the foundational importance of doctrine.
2. The beginning of 1 Timothy 4 presents the challenges of proclaiming Christ amid cultural pressures.
3. 1 Timothy 4:6–14 reminds church leadership of their priorities.
4. Chapter 4 concludes with a recognition of the need for pastoral diligence and accountability as well as what is at stake when a pastor's character is in question.

Truly consider memorizing this passage. Reading through these verses and meditating on them is of much value, but memorizing them is an even greater benefit. By memorizing them you will soak this truth into your mind so that this Spirit-illuminated Word will become a living part of your thoughts and conversations throughout a pastoral search.

Repeat these truths to remember them. If you prayerfully memorize the words of 1 Timothy 4:6–16 and repeat them a modest 2–300 times, you will be amazed at how they find expression in your prayers and interviews. In so doing, you will see the Spirit-illuminated Word lead your pastoral search.

Chris Brauns is the senior pastor at the Red Brick Church in Stillman Valley, Illinois. He has served in pastoral ministry for over twenty years and is the author of *Unpacking Forgiveness*, *When the Word Leads Your Pastoral Search*, and *Bound Together*.

GAIN THE LEGIT FACTOR

The fruit of the Spirit is . . .
– Galatians 5:22

By now you should have put together almost everything you'll send to churches during the initial phase of your job search. To wit, you're smokin' the curve.

As my coach used to tell us, it's important in the early stages of a race to not look down, to stay in our lane, and to keep our strides long. In the context of a job search, this means you must develop a system for tracking your progress, and you must understand how to talk about previous transitions. In addition, you'll need to understand the goal behind much of the professionalism I'm advocating for in gaining the "legit factor."

Keep Track of Everything

Like so many other aspects of the job search, the complexity will depend on your context. If you're currently established in a ministry role and only casually looking for a job, your search will likely not be too involved, and you'll manage it without much effort.

If, however, you're in a transition stage, say, about to graduate from seminary, then it's easy to get overwhelmed. The job search is a hydra; the more you attack it, the more of a beast it becomes. Establish a system of tracking everything from the beginning because, at some point, you'll forget which church you sent which piece of information, which church has a deadline coming up, and which church has a senior pastor who prefers to be called Steve, not Steven or Stephen. One pastor learned this the hard, embarrassing way. Before getting a tracking system in place, he accidentally applied for a job twice, with the second time coming after he had already received a "no." Oops.

Let me give you an analogy. During the last few years I've developed several food allergies that have caused a lot of discomfort. Some days it even left me unable to work. I don't know why this happened, and I'm not happy about it, but it did. In order to figure out what I was allergic to, I had to track everything I ate for several months. At first I would convince myself I could wait until the end of the day, or even wait several days, to record everything I had eaten. I thought this would be more efficient.

Big surprise: this didn't work. I always forgot the details.

It's the same in the job search. You think you can keep track of it, but you can't. So make a folder, electronic or otherwise, for every job and keep track of every interaction. Don't wait a day or two. You'll forget.

I recently went back and looked at my computer folder entitled "placement." It was from when I was preparing to graduate from seminary. There were seventeen different folders in it! Granted, some were threadbare because I only had one or two interactions with a church, but other folders were stuffed with details. Another pastor, when he was searching for a job, used a three-folder system (apply, applied, rejected) as well as an Excel spreadsheet for information about when he had contacted people and other pertinent information. Along with folders, you should create a calendar to remind you of important deadlines and when you need to follow up with a church.

If You Are in a Different Country, Work Extra Hard

If you're applying for a job outside of your country, please know you have a massive hurdle to overcome, both financially and logistically. Small things like conducting a phone interview become more complicated. Think about what this will mean for the church that hires you. For example, consider the expense to fly you in for the interview and to relocate you. Be prepared to discuss these factors. This is not to say you wouldn't be worth it; you probably have much to offer, especially by way of perspective, but these are the realities any international candidate will have to face.

Here are a few tips to overcoming these extra factors. Have someone from the country you're trying to move to look over your material before you send it. Also, if you have references in the country, put them down. Highlight any and all connections you have. Your extra attention to detail in these areas will show a church that you're serious about the job, which will help you gain more credibility.

Make the Follow-Up Phone Call

After you send your e-mail, call the church to tell them you're interested. I'm tempted to say you should call even if their job description paperwork says "don't call." I say this because you want to stand out. True, you'll be disregarding their stated preferences, but I look at it like this: The search team could be sifting through two hundred packets, and when they come to your packet you want the search team to have heard from someone, maybe the church secretary saying, "Hey, *this* guy called a few days ago and sounded really nice and really interested in the job."

Know what you're going to say on the call. Keep it short and sweet. You're just saying a quick hello to let them know how interested you are and what specifically attracted you to the job and the church. If you'd like, you might even ask a question such as, "What do you love about your church?"

Stay Positive Regarding Previous Job Transitions

When writing or speaking about previous transitions, it's important to speak positively during the early stages of your job search. You should stress the positive reasons you're looking for a job. For example, if part of why you're leaving is because there was a change in senior leadership and you no longer fit in, don't go into all of that in your cover letter. There's probably a place for that; it's just not there. So for now, keep things upbeat.

Know Whom, When, and in What Order to Tell People You Are Taking a New Job

Few things have the potential to harm relationships like finding out important information from the wrong person or at the wrong time. If your girlfriend decided to break up with you, but she told a bunch of other people first, you're not going to forget it.

Likewise, it's important to think through the details related to announcing your transition from the church. When done well, transitions can and should be celebrated, not merely endured.

Therefore, when you know you'll be taking a new job—or you very likely might be taking a new job—you'll also want to know whom to tell, how soon to tell them, and in what order. This means you'll have to understand what's appropriate in your current ministry context. Are you about to graduate from Bible college? If so, this will look very different than if you're the lead pastor of a mega-church. Cionca writes:

> A good transition begins with a healthful, edifying resignation. Rather than shocking the congregation with an announcement from the pulpit, many pastors have found it beneficial to notify the members in writing. A letter mailed on Monday morning will reach most congregants by Wednesday. People will then have several days to process their feelings before hearing any public

statement. This procedure also provides time to notify key leaders and close friends personally while the letters are en route.[1]

When I was completing seminary, figuring out when and whom to
tell wasn't difficult. The church I attended was a good church, but it
didn't have a full-time position open, nor would it in the foreseeable
future. Therefore, it was easy for me to talk openly about job opportunities. It made for an encouraging season as I could share prayer
requests and job updates publicly.

Many contexts don't allow for such openness. You'll need to consider how others before you have left and how the church treated
them when they did. This is hard to generalize given the particulars of
every departure, but if there's a precedent for pastors being let go as
soon as their boss knows they're interested in leaving, then this
should affect when you tell the leadership. On the other hand, if the
church has a history of being gracious and understanding amid mutually beneficial transitions, then it's likely your approach will be very
different.

When it's time to tell others, consider doing so in terms of concen-
trically expanding circles. The first inner circle might consist of key
leadership. Perhaps this is your senior pastor and the elder board. The
next circle may include ministry friends or those with whom you
worked closely. Finally, the last circle involves the congregation and
those outside your church. If you tell people in this order, I believe
you'll be doing what you can to respect those around you.

When it comes time to make your announcement public, go out of
your way to tell as many people as you can in person, especially those
with whom you are close. The last thing you want is someone you're
close with to find out you're leaving when they open the weekly
church bulletin.

My advice in this book is mostly about how to maximize your experience inside the typical hiring box rather than to help you navigate
a hiring process outside the norms. I'll leave it to others to reinvent
the wheel. You may find yourself in far more ideal situations than
most. For example, in a 9Marks Journal issue dedicated to the topic of

---

[1] Cionca, *Before You Move*, 198.

pastoral transitions, there's an interview with Michael Lawrence about his then-recent transition from Capitol Hill Baptist Church.[2] Aspects of Lawrence's transition are beautiful and, if you ask me, aspects of it are outlandish. It's beautiful in that both churches eschewed secrecy. When the search team came to Capitol Hill Baptist to interview Lawrence, there was no secrecy. Capitol Hill Baptist had the visiting search team stand up in the service so they could be prayed for and so members could know who to speak with if they wished to communicate something about Lawrence. If such transparency is possible in a given context—and it apparently was in theirs—then this sounds wonderfully healthy.

But it also sounds outlandish. I can't imagine many churches allowing this. And the way the interview reads, it's held up as a model. The article is titled "How to Leave Your Church Well." At one point Lawrence makes the statement, "One way to leave your church poorly is to spring it on your congregation. You show up one Sunday and tell them that next Sunday is the last Sunday that their beloved pastor is going to be there."[3] I agree, but these are not the only two options; they are the two extremes.

What if Lawrence had decided not to leave his current church or the new church had decided not to call him? This could have happened for a number of reasons, many of them benign. I supposed no damage would have been done. But what if this level of transparency occurred when three more churches came looking for him? It wouldn't be long before this became intolerable. And what if several associate pastors were doing this in a given year? Consider the toll on that local church. And what if Lawrence was not an associate pastor, but the lead pastor? That's a different thing too.

When Lawrence accepted the call, which was in October, he told the church he wouldn't come until the following August and wouldn't begin preaching until October. That's nine months until arrival and twelve months until preaching. He wanted his children to finish the school year, and he wanted to learn the local culture before preaching

---

[2] "How to Leave Your Church Well: An Interview with Michael Lawrence," *9Marks Journal* (Jan.–Feb. 2011), 5–8.
[3] Ibid., 7.

to them. I'll confess that I'm almost envious of this boldness, this root-edness in God to make such requests. I can learn something from it. But at the same time, if I'm reading his questions rightly, the interviewer seems slightly incredulous about this detail. "And you told them that, even though you were coming in August, you wouldn't start preaching until October?" he asks. "That's right," Lawrence answers.[4]

A hire like this isn't feasible in most churches, not necessarily because of a spiritual weakness but because they don't have as deep a bench or as long a track record of sending out pastors to other churches. This transition is unusual, and wonderfully so. But precisely because it's so unusual, I hesitate to hold it out as a model or a norm.

Instead, my aim is to help the typical pastor in the typical church to do the best he can. I won't prescribe exactly how this should look in your given context. In every transition—both the typical and the atypical—our goal should be to love individuals, consider the local church, and guard God's reputation. If you're out only to protect your own interests, then you're in sin (Phil 2:4–5). If, however, you seek to love others and honor God, more often than not your transition will be a season of encouragement for yourself, your family, and the churches involved.

Gain the Legit Factor

Let's close this chapter by highlighting one of the fundamental goals behind everything I've said so far. As a candidate, the goal of your resume and cover letter—professional formatting, thoughtful references, and expressions of your eagerness—is to gain the legit factor.

What do I mean by "legit factor"? To be blunt, it means the potential employer knows you're not a chump. It means your Christian faith is sincere; it's legit. It means there's not a disconnect between your public life and your private life. If you're married, it means you love your spouse and aren't headed for divorce. The legit factor tells the search committee you won't blow up their church in a power struggle. It means your life not only displays the *gifting* of the Spirit but also the *fruit* of the Spirit: love, joy, peace, patience, kindness, goodness,

---

[4] Ibid., 6.

faithfulness, gentleness, and self-control (cf., Matt 7:21–23 with Gal 5:22–23). A mature, thoughtful, and godly church doesn't care how wonderfully you can preach if your character is cancerous on the inside. Eventually the real you—the real us—always comes out. In other words, a good search committee has the difficult job of discerning between gold and iron pyrite.

This is why the qualifications for eldership preclude recent converts: "He must not be a recent convert, or he may become puffed up with conceit and fall into the condemnation of the devil" (1 Tim 3:6). Paul doesn't say a new convert can't perform the visible aspects of pastoring. He implies that when he does the job well, a young man won't likely have the character to stay humble.

Consider the example of King Saul. If ever there was a person who was impressive, not only on paper but in person, it was Saul. "There was a man of Benjamin whose name was Kish . . . a man of wealth. And he had a son whose name was Saul, a handsome young man. There was not a man among the people of Israel more handsome than he. From his shoulders upward he was taller than any of the people" (1 Sam 9:1–2).

Wealthy, handsome, and tall. "So can this Saul guy preach?" a near-sighted search committee might ask. "Because if he can, we have a winner." Joseph Umidi writes, "The most often repeated survey response from pastors and pastors-to-be in our research is that search committees focus on the wrong characteristics, such as personality, appearance, poise, and charisma, rather than discerning the real heart of the person."[5]

Of course, we know the whole story of Saul. What begins with excitement ends in tragedy. That's because character always trumps appearance and competency in the long run.

This is why growing and leveraging your personal network (which I'll talk about in the next chapter) is so important in the hiring process. If the church knows someone who will vouch for your character, then the real journey can begin.

---

[5] Joseph L. Umidi, *Confirming the Pastoral Call: A Guide to Matching Candidates and Congregations* (Grand Rapids, MI: Kregel, 2000), 53.

Consider also how the legit factor played out in the life of another man in the Bible who, incidentally, was also named Saul (at least originally). When Saul of Tarsus became Paul the apostle, we might say he had a hard time in the job-search process. This is understandable. Proving you love Christians is a hard sell when you formerly killed them. "Lord," said Ananias, "I have heard from many about this man how much evil he has done to your saints at Jerusalem" (Acts 9:13). But things began to look up for Paul when Barnabas, whom the early church thought well of (4:36–37), vouched for him (9:27). This was no small thing.

If you're not able to establish the legit factor through your personal network, don't despair. There are other things you can do. Churches often hire men and women they haven't previously known. As I mentioned in the preface, that's why I've written this book, and I hope it's why you're reading it. I don't want qualified and godly pastors to flounder during the hiring process. Instead, I want to help them find good churches where they can use their gifts. And if you're following the strategies mentioned so far, hopefully you're well on your way to smoking the curve.

*   *   *

"Your Calling Is More Than Your Paycheck: Don't Rule Out Bi-Vocational Ministry"

By Chase Replogle

No one dreams of someday becoming a bi-vocational pastor with a 9-5 side hustle. I sure didn't. Through Bible college and seminary, I had all kinds of ideas about the church I would pastor: the building, the preaching, the programs, the sermon graphics, the passionately engaged and talented congregants showing up punctually each week.

The churches we imagine so easily construct themselves on the scaffolding of our best curation, never plagued by reality but aided in the limitless potential of abstraction, the best bits and pieces we've collected always forming together into what we proudly call our calling—a pastor and his church. No one has to add full-time, salaried, with retirement benefits and reserved parking. It's what we most naturally imagine when we use the word pastor.

Imagination and ambition are a part of every occupation, but given the proximity to holy and eternal things, pastors may be most prone to dream. I was, but my dream wasn't panning out. Seven years into a church plant, it hadn't gone exactly according to plan.

Our church started in a home basement, twenty or so people gathering on Sunday nights for food and Scripture. Before long, we gave it a name and rented space at a local community center. I started to draw a paycheck. It was about one-fifth of the income I needed to pay our monthly bills and put gas in our cars. I had to find additional work, but we sensed God was doing something. So, we continued.

In seminary I got interested in web development—I've always had an impractical curiosity. Alongside courses in Greek and Hebrew, I taught myself PHP, CSS, HTML, and Javascript. I started building websites for a few friends and churches. The work continued to grow. In fact, the web work grew faster than the church did. What had once been only curiosity was quickly turning into a career and also a predicament.

I was called to be a pastor, not a web designer. I was supposed to become Moses, not Zuckerberg. I was terrified that allowing web design to become my full-time job was like Moses deciding to cash in on building Nile riverboats while moonlighting the whole exodus thing on the side. How could I call myself a pastor if nearly everyone knew me as a web designer? I felt like I was losing my calling.

Calling and vocation are words we throw around, I think, without really understanding them. We live in a world that only knows how to appraise specialization and expertise. You're allowed one calling—one vocation—anything more creates a fraction, and fractions are always a compromise, a sacrifice of real potential.

We too often confuse vocation and career. The word vocation comes from an old Latin word meaning "to be called." Career, by alternative, comes from the Latin for a "wheeled vehicle," literally, a wheel barrel. A career is a task, a pile of dirt that needs to be moved from one place to another, and hopefully someone is willing to pay you to do it. I mean no disrespect toward the work. There is great dignity in it, and it's this kind that I have spent most of my life doing. But a vocation is something far more wholistic than a timecard. Your life is made up of countless vocations, a patchwork of callings: spouse, parent, child, neighbor, citizen, hobbyist, friend, employee, follower of Christ, and, for some, pastor. No one's life is ever a single calling.

So here it is: what I really want you to see is that your calling is not primarily defined by how you pay back student loans or purchase groceries. These are simply the logistics of life. A calling is something far more comprehensive. Your career doesn't have to define that calling. There is room for a calling and a career.

When I finally came to this realization, something profound happened. I realized that the mark of a pastor was not his paycheck. It meant I could carve out a pastoral vocation supported by, and in my case improved by, outside work. With a paycheck secured, being a pastor took on a reenergized set of priorities: personally knowing the people in my congregation, preparing myself to lead them in Scripture and worship, and cultivating time for prayer. That work can be fit into life beyond a 9-5.

It means most nights you'll find me with a commentary instead of Netflix. It means we host a lot of meals in our home with church members. And it means I prioritize prayer, forcing me to involve a lot of volunteers for tasks other pastors might find in their job descriptions. But at the end of each week—closing our services in prayer, chatting with couples in the lobby, hauling my son with me to hospital visitations—I still feel like a pastor.

It's not perfect, and certainly not void of stress, but pastoring never is. I think Paul would have offered similar advice as he did for marriage. If you're married, great. If you're single, great. Is your church able to pay you a full-time salary? Great. Do you find yourself having to work outside the church? Great.

The real work is not figuring out a path to the lustrous, full-time image you've previously imagined. The real work is recognizing what God is doing and receiving each invitation with vocational gratitude. Dreaming about what you wished ministry looked like is robbing you of what God is doing right in front of you. God alone knows where your career and callings will lead you, but I do know this, the joy is in faithfulness. The dignity of being a pastor is earned in faithfulness, not in a salary. Don't rule out how God might use another career to make you a better pastor.

> The only opportunity you will ever have to live by faith is in the circumstances you are provided this very day: this house you live in, this family you find yourself in, this job you have been given, the weather conditions that prevail at the . . . moment.
>
> — Eugene Peterson, *Run with the Horses:*
> *The Quest for Life at Its Best*

Chase Replogle is the pastor of Bent Oak Church, a freelance web designer, and the host of the *Pastor Writer* podcast. He has a degree in biblical studies and an M.A. in New Testament. A native of the Ozark woods, he enjoys being outdoors with his wife and two kids: fly-fishing, playing the mandolin (badly), and quail hunting with his bird dog Millie.

NETWORK AND SEARCH FOR OPENINGS

You are fellow citizens with the saints and
members of the household of God.
– Ephesians 2:19

When you own a car but you're not, shall we say, a *car guy*, you're often at the mercy of a mechanic.

I hate this feeling. Sure, I know the basics—you're not getting me to buy "blinker fluid." But when you start talking about the mechanical guts of a car, I'm lost. This is why in every city I move to I always try to find someone who knows a trustworthy mechanic. It makes a huge difference. It's a lot easier to swallow an $800 bill from a mechanic you trust because you know that bill is fair and the work is actually needed to keep the car safe for your family. Your mind is at ease because you know the mechanic is legit. And you know this because you know your friend who recommended him.

The process I go through to find a mechanic (also called networking), is something like the process you'll want to go through to find a job in ministry.

Build and Leverage Your Personal Network

Statistics regarding how people land jobs are difficult to come by because job searches, especially the effective ones, incorporate multiple strategies: cold calls, online job boards, staffing firms, and networking. Moreover, where general stats from the business world can be found, it's difficult to predict their carryover into ministry. Still, it would seem networking is by far the most fruitful strategy; some claim it's responsible for over half of all placements.[1]

A Greasy Process

But for whatever reason, I hate the word networking. It feels greasy. When I hear it, I think cheap suits, slick hair, gaudy gold chains, and a guy who points with his index finger as he talks.[2] Even if this is a cliché, at one point or another, we've all had the miserable experience of being used. I call it networking after Genesis 3, east of Eden.

Recently our church magically had a new couple show up about the time we were hiring for a new position. This couple came in hot and heavy, volunteering for this, attending that. Things seemed promising but still not altogether right. After a week or so, the man applied for the job. He wasn't the right person for the job, but we thought it respectful to let him take a shot. Besides, maybe we were wrong about him.

We weren't.

Over the next four weeks, our initial suspicions were confirmed. We graciously relayed the news to the couple that he wouldn't get the job, but we were still committed to finding a meaningful place for them to serve. They blew off calls and e-mails, and two weeks later they were gone, with divots needing to be replaced in the ministries they said they would serve. I found out months later that they immediately went down the road to another church—which also had a job

---

[1] Cf., Orville Pierson, *The Unwritten Rules of the Highly Effective Job Search,* 23, 61–67, 178. Also, J. E. Eubanks found that 67 percent of the people who responded to his survey "made initial contact with the ministry they eventually accepted a call from through networking" (*From M.Div. to Rev.,* 69).

[2] Proverbs puts it this way: "A worthless person, a wicked man, goes about with crooked speech, winks with his eyes, signals with his feet, points with his finger" (6:12–13).

opening—where they lied about what happened at our church and badmouthed us to that pastor (who is also a friend).

This is networking *after* Genesis 3. One pastor described his feelings about it like this: "I hate networking . . . The thought of me saying, 'Let me form some kind of bond-relationship with you for the expressed purpose of you connecting me with a local job near you,' is an anathema to me." But this pastor quickly added, "And yet, of the three jobs that I've had, two of them came because I knew someone in the church."

So what if networking didn't have to be greasy? What might networking have looked like *before* the fall?

A Good and Godly Process

Imagine what it would be like if networking were more like buying a friend a cup of coffee than trying to sell a used car.

At its best, networking should be nothing more than purposeful communication with people you care about and people who care about you. Anyone can create a list of friends and acquaintances who want to see them find a job where they'd thrive. I bet you can too. Besides, if there's anywhere networking is appropriate, it's among Christians. Consider how the New Testament speaks of us: the body of Christ, the household and family of God, the vine and the branches, the sheep of God's flock. What do these all share? Interconnectedness.[3]

Make Your List

Make a list of everyone you think would be excited to see you in the right job. Some will be your close friends and family. Others you might hardly know, though they might know about potential jobs. Consider putting that pastor of that large church in the large city you want to move to on your list. Perhaps add someone in the placement department of a seminary or someone in an administrative role of a denomination.

If you're in seminary, send a follow-up e-mail to outside speakers who come to your school to share chapel messages. You don't have to

---

[3] Eubanks, *From M.Div. to Rev.*, 56–57.

send a long e-mail, just something that says thanks for coming and why you appreciated his or her message. One student I know asked his seminary if he could be a driver for outside chapel speakers and made many good relationships in the process.

If you're not in seminary, you can do this when you attend conferences or denominational gatherings. If the speaker sends you a return e-mail, you'll have a list of people who you might be able to call someday when it's time to look for a job. Of course, the more popular the speaker and the larger the conference, the less likely you'll be to get a reply.

The point, though, isn't to get "big" connections but helpful ones. Often a pastor with strong regional but not national connections will be just as helpful, if not more helpful. And whether you're in seminary or not, when a book impacts you, reach out to the author with a short note sharing why you found the work so helpful.

Keep Making Your Lists

I keep talking about a networking list, but let me be clearer. There are actually *two* lists. In the first, you're just brainstorming about those who you think *could* help you in this process. On this list, you should put every pastor, every lay elder, and every denominational contact you know. Add a few of the seminary professors you knew best and anyone else you think might be able to help.

The next step is to speak with these people and ask if they'd mind being on an e-mail list of individuals you want to send periodic updates to regarding the progress of your job search. This is your actual networking list. It can be overwhelming when you look at it. If you feel this way, Brian D. Krueger advises, "Set a personal goal to make at least one . . . networking contact per day."[4] As you do this, start with the "easiest" contacts first, those people who won't be hard to call and will gladly help. This will help get the ball rolling.

---

[4] Brian D. Krueger, *The College Grad Job Hunter: Insider Techniques and Tactics for Finding a Top-Paying Job*, 6th Edition (Avon, MA: Adams Media, 2008), 83.

As you speak to people, be sure to give a length of time as to how long you expect to send e-mail updates. You might say something like this:

> For the next nine months, I'm going to e-mail some updates to friends about my job-search progress. Would it be okay if I e-mailed you an update about once every two weeks during this time?[5]

> Also, would you be open to sending me any ideas or leads you might have for me?

> And would you mind praying for me as you think about my situation?

This is something most people will say yes to because they know what they're getting into. It's been made clear to them that you're not expecting them to find the job for you—just to help.

Before moving on, let me mention three more things about networking. First, in your preliminary phone call to someone in your network (and in every subsequent e-mail), remember to emphasize the level of confidentiality needed. Are they sworn to secrecy? Or are they able and encouraged to forward your e-mail around to their friends? The answer will depend on your situation, but make sure it's abundantly clear.

Second, keep your initial e-mails short, especially if you don't know the person well. "Anything more than one hundred words from a stranger seems downright presumptuous."[6] Moreover, in the age of smartphones, it's helpful to send e-mails that can be read without having to scroll . . . and scroll . . . and . . . I'm done. *Delete.*

Lastly, when you e-mail your personal network, consider using the Bcc (blind carbon copy) function. This way individual email addresses remain private. This might not seem like a big deal, but here's

---

[5] "If you are actively pursuing employment, it's best to contact [your network] once every two weeks. If you are passively seeking employment, once every one or two months is sufficient" (Ibid., 83).

[6] Steve Dalton, *The 2-Hour Job Search: Using Technology to Get the Right Job Faster* (Berkeley, CA: Ten Speed, 2012), 109.

what you don't want: you don't want your dear Aunt Beatrice (bless her heart) to keep hitting "reply to all" to tell you how excited she is for you. Not professional. So avoid this by using Bcc for your emails.

If your e-mail list gets really large, you might even want to use a bulk e-mail service such as MailChimp (which may be free for the size we're talking about). The upside of a bulk e-mail service is that your e-mail will look professional, but make sure to keep a personal tone in the writing so it doesn't come across like a form letter. It's a hard thing to balance, but if your motives for networking are pure, people will sense this and be glad to lend a hand.

Be Intentional on Your Social Media, Blog, and Website

As soon as anyone takes you seriously as a candidate, they will Google you, and when they do, they'll follow the breadcrumbs to your social media pages, blog, or website.

Think about this every time you post something. If you're inclined to post photos of the steak dinner you are about to eat on Facebook, that's probably fine. If, however, you're given to posting links about your love for those either on the right or left politically and theologically, scale it back. Here's the general principle: anything you don't want a search committee to see, don't post.

I should also say something specifically about the social media platform LinkedIn, both because of its popularity and because of its aim to be a helpful business-networking site. In fact, many career-building and job-search books have whole sections devoted to telling go-getters how they might optimize this tool for personal benefit. Moreover, if you looked on Amazon.com right now, you'd see plenty of books devoted entirely to LinkedIn.

So how can a pastor make use of this platform?

I'd encourage you to create a profile, or if you already have one, to update and expand it. You should do this whether you intend to make use of it or not. Search teams may check it, and outdated information might confuse them.

While LinkedIn is a useful tool, don't get your hopes up that it will land you a job in ministry. It's my impression that, though many pastors have a LinkedIn account, they rarely check it. If you have an account but never fully set it up and you don't intend to, then it's better to delete the account than to have a blank avatar where a picture belongs.

As for Pinterest, Google+, Snap Chat, Tumblr—and whatever other social media platforms exist—none of these will help get you a job either. One colleague did tell me, however, that he has had good success using Twitter as a networking tool *after* he's met a person in real life. But for the most part, if you use social media, do so because you enjoy it and see a benefit to it. And as you use it, make sure what you post will not prevent you from getting a job.

Know Where to Find Other Job Openings

Having clear and professional documents makes for a good start. And yet, if you don't know where to send them, you're not going to get a job. You must connect your information with the right opportunity. Ideally, such opportunities would come through your personal network.

But what if my network is weak? And what if, regardless of the size of my network, the opportunities still don't come? Then where do I look for job openings? No need to worry. There are many places to look. Here are a few.

Job-Search Websites

Church Staffing[7] tends to be the best place to look, as it seems to be the most populated. But there are other places as well, such as Church Staff Search[8] and Church Jobs Online.[9] The quality, however, decreases quickly after these. The top websites do receive a lot of traffic and thus,

---

[7] churchstaffing.com.
[8] churchstaffsearch.com.
[9] churchjobsonline.com.

competition, so keep in mind you'll likely have to move quickly and be very determined if you find a job you're interested in.

Vanderbloemen Search Group,[10] The Slingshot Group,[11] and The Shepherd's Staff[12] are all pastor-recruitment firms for churches (i.e., headhunting firms). They also have job postings. If you talk with a hiring firm directly or end up working with one because you're talking with a church that's hired one, remember that recruitment firms work for and are paid by the church, not the candidate. The firm typically retains between 25 and 40 percent of the pastor's first-year salary-plus-housing as well as travel expenses.[13] But working with a search firm isn't to be feared, as though the church will be reducing your salary to compensate. Having another motivated party involved should mitigate risk for both candidate and church.[14]

Additionally, The Gospel Coalition, a favorite organization of mine, has an online job board.[15] It's stuffed with opportunities.

Denominations

Often church denominations have resources for connecting candidates and churches; they have a vested interest in doing so. I'm thinking of official denominations such as the Presbyterian Church in America[16] or the Southern Baptist Convention.[17] But I also have in mind church movements like Sovereign Grace[18] that are not official denominations.

---

[10] vanderbloemen.com/featured-jobs.

[11] slingshotgroup.org/job_posting.

[12] theshepherdsstaff.com/job-postings.

[13] William Vanderbloemen and Warren Bird, *Next: Pastoral Succession that Works* (Grand Rapids, MI: Baker, 2014), 162.

[14] Something to consider when working with a search firm is that if they do present you to one of the churches who contracted them, you should expect to be evaluated with only a few other candidates. That's how it works. The church is paying the firm to have only the best candidates brought to them. Therefore, the typical interviewing that happens early in a pastoral search won't occur with individual churches but instead will happen with the search firm. What this means for your heart is that you'll need to be prepared to parachute into the search process far deeper than normal and with a higher potential to be disappointed. I know one pastor who, over the course of four months working with the search firm, was rejected by six churches, and in each rejection, there were only a few other candidates. That hurts.

[15] jobs.thegospelcoalition.org/.

[16] pcaac.org/get-involved/non-pastoral-job-positions.

[17] sbc.net/jobs.

[18] sovereigngrace.com.

I can't speak with authority concerning every denomination or movement, but I can speak to my own, The Evangelical Free Church of America (EFCA). Our movement divides the U.S. into seventeen districts, and each district with its own staff who support, on average, one hundred churches. We also host a job search website that attempts to match churches and candidates. It typically has eighty jobs and two hundred candidates, which is actually a very high ratio.

When I was in seminary and looking for a job, I sent cover letters and resumes to someone in each district and followed up with a phone call. For me, this didn't generate many leads, but I think if I had already been serving full-time in an EFCA church and especially if I had already been ordained and not fresh out of seminary, speaking with district superintendents would have opened more doors.

Church-Planting Networks

If you're interested in church planting, then you probably already know about organizations such as Acts 29,[19] Sojourn Network,[20] Converge (formerly the Baptist General Conference),[21] Sovereign Grace,[22] the Association of Relational Churches (ARC),[23] The North American Mission Board (SEND),[24] and others. You'll find them if you look. In fact, some seminaries, such as Midwestern Baptist Theological Seminary, even have a church planting coordinator on staff.

Bible Colleges and Seminaries

Some of the best places to find jobs are through Bible colleges and seminaries. In such cases, the upside is twofold. First, by virtue of each institution's theological DNA, the theology of the churches is already vetted, at least to some extent. This is helpful to both you and the churches. Second, churches often have staff members who are positively biased to hiring candidates from their alma mater. There's nothing wrong with this. For both candidate and church, the hiring

---

[19] acts29.com.
[20] sojournnetwork.com.
[21] converge.org.
[22] sovereigngrace.com/church-planting.
[23] arcchurches.com.
[24] namb.net/church-planting.

process is a risk, and anything one can do to mitigate that risk, including connecting people who shared theology professors, is a good thing.

The downside of finding jobs through Bible colleges and seminaries, however, is that often access is only granted to current students and alumni. Under certain circumstances, the gatekeeper will give you access. To find this gatekeeper, just call the school and ask to speak with the person overseeing placement or find him or her on the seminary's website. If this leads to a dead end, perhaps ask friends to see if they can get lists from their respective seminaries.

Other Ministry Organizations

Most of you are pastors looking to connect with a local church. Some of you, however, may be thinking more broadly. I won't list many specifics here but likely every major mission agency, camp, and parachurch organization has their own job postings. This is true for places like Fellowship of Christian Athletes,[25] Cru (formerly Campus Crusade for Christ),[26] and Gospel for Asia.[27]

Networking can be an overwhelming project. Don't get discouraged. If you stay at it the leads will come and you'll be faced with a whole new set of questions.

*   *   *

"When You Hear 'No'"

By Jeremy Writebol

As I sat across the table from the lead pastor of a hiring church, I expected him to articulate how much he was looking forward to having me on the team and how dynamic my leadership would be at their church. In many ways, the interview process and expediency of it was building an expectation within my mind that I would be

---

[25] teamfca.org.
[26] cru.org/opportunities/careers.
[27] gfa.org/joinstaff.

offered the job. Why else would they run this fast through the process with me? Surely they had found their guy.

But it was with half a bite of burger in my mouth that the undesired and fatal verdict was spoken. "Jeremy, you're a nice guy, but honestly you are a huge risk for what we need on our leadership team right now. I don't think you'd be a good fit here. We're going to have to say no, but thank you for walking with us through this process." The burger felt like lead in my stomach at that point. I had been told "no," and the search process for my dream job was over.

Yes, I'll admit that I was very disappointed to hear "no," but over the years (and after many more "nos") I've come to see that hearing a "no" is not necessarily a denial of your skill and gifting as much as it is a gift from God to keep you on the path of faith, trusting that he is the one who ordains our places and paths in ministry. While rejections can be deflating, they can also be a means of grace whereby God guides you to a season of ministry that better fits your gifting and competence in ministry. Here are three lessons I've found to be helpful for my heart after hearing a "no."

Believe the gospel. First, I must believe the gospel. It's tempting to let our identities get wrapped up in our vocations. We can build our hearts on the approval of others. Not being offered a position we sought after can chip away at our self-built identities and affirmations. This is why we need to deeply remember the gospel.

The gospel reminds us that our identity and value aren't built on what we do or the titles we possess. Christ is our hope—not the dream job we've pursued. We are no less sons and daughters of God through faith in Christ because we were not hired and heard a Divine "no." As the hymn writer Edward Mote taught us to sing, "My hope is built on nothing less than Jesus' blood and righteousness." Believe that good news!

Minister right where you are. Remember the man in the Bible who applied for Jesus's school of discipleship almost immediately after being healed from demon possession? He was ready to follow Jesus anywhere and do anything for him. Personally, I would have thought this man was the ideal candidate for my ministry school. The healed man was passionate, available, and loyal. Yet Jesus told him "no."

Instead, the man was instructed to stay at home and tell his community how God had been merciful to him. In the midst of receiving a "no," he was redirected to labor for the gospel right where he'd always been (see Mark 5:18–20).

Hearing a "no" from one church doesn't mean we should quit the ministry. Rather, it helps us to be active and faithful right where God has us currently. In the divine providence of God, the work he has placed right in front of us is more pressing than the dreams of greener pastures and more influential platforms of ministry that we might have been longing to be commissioned into. Hearing a "no" should refocus us on the task at hand.

Depend on God. The most challenging thing about hearing a "no" is trying to figure out why we were not offered a desired position. Our motivations can feel pure and our goals right in wanting to glorify God and use our gifts for the building of the kingdom, but when we hear a "no" we are often frustrated that God isn't apparently on the same page with us.

If we believe that God orders our steps (Ps 139:16) and that he has prepared good works ahead of time for us to do (Eph 2:10), then we can rest confident that a "no" is ultimately for our good and for his glory. If our heavenly Father only gives good gifts, then we can trust his gracious hand to send us exactly where he sees fit to glorify himself and advance his gospel. The goodness of God has not abandoned us.

Looking for a ministry position is one of the most difficult vocational actions, but it is superintended by a loving God for our good. The "nos" are hard to hear, but it is these hard providences that cause us to look all the more for his glad smile.

Jeremy Writebol serves as the lead campus pastor of Woodside Bible Church in Plymouth, Michigan, and is the Executive Director of *Gospel-Centered Discipleship*. He is also an author and contributor to several books including *everPresent* and *Make, Mature, Multiply*.

PART TWO

MAKING *The* MOVE

DON'T *Just* SEND A RESUME

UNDERSTAND THE HIRING PROCESS

This is why I left you in Crete, so that you might put what remained
into order, and appoint elders in every town as I directed you.
– Titus 1:5

Okay, so you have your resume and references together, and you're actually talking with churches. So far, you're out of the starting blocks fast and clean; you've smoked the curve.

Now what? How do you prepare for interviews? How do you know if a church will be a good fit? And what about money—is it okay to talk about that?

To land a job you must think strategically along the way. That's what these next chapters are about. In this one, we'll talk about the typical process involved in hiring a pastor.

But first, there's something you should be aware of, especially if you're applying for the role of senior pastor. In all likelihood, the church you're interested in wasn't planning on hiring you . . . or anyone. Carolyn Weese and J. Russell Crabtree, who spent many years studying pastoral transitions, estimate that "less than 1 percent of all churches operate by a strategic plan that includes the pastoral transition as an element of that plan."[1] In short, *uh-oh*.

This means 99 percent of the time the church wasn't planning on their pastor leaving. Now they're looking for someone new, not because they *wanted to* hire a new pastor but because they *have to*.

I don't mean to scare or deter you, though I do want you to think soberly about pastoral transition. If you have this information in the back of your mind, it may help explain why a church handles the process with less professionalism or enthusiasm than you'd expect or desire.

Their lack of professionalism could be because they just don't have much practice and the person who knew how to conduct a pastoral search is the one who left. Robert Dingman, a former professional consultant to search committees, notes, "A major problem with most search committees is that they are always comprised of amateurs and usually beginners."[2] Therefore, their so-called unprofessional tactics might not be tactics at all. They're volunteers sifting through applications between bites of pizza on their lunch break. They're shoehorning a reference check into their schedule after their kids are asleep and just before they crash for the night.

And perhaps their lack of enthusiasm is because they're navigating controversy regarding the departure of the previous pastor. "When a pastor leaves a church, members and friends will have varying emotions to deal with."[3] They may experience denial, anger, depression, and even anxiety over the future of the church and their role within it.

None of this should necessarily stop you from joining their church. One or two years after your arrival, a healthy church, or at least a church making progress toward health, is a real possibility.

---

[1] Carolyn Weese and J. Russell Crabtree, *The Elephant in the Boardroom: Speaking the Unspoken about Pastoral Transitions* (San Francisco: Jossey-Bass, 2004), 134.

[2] Robert W. Dingman, *In Search of a Leader: The Complete Search Committee Guidebook* (Westlake Village, CA: Lakeside Books, 1989), 144.

[3] John Vonhof, *Pastoral Search: The Alban Guide to Managing the Pastoral Search Process* (The Alban Institute, 1999), 18.

Know How a Church Will Hire You

If you live in rural Pennsylvania, consider what you need to do to go on a vacation to Los Angeles. Do you know *how* you'll get there? Will you fly? Will you drive? And if you drive, will you stay in hotels, at campsites, or with friends? Will you make a sightseeing road trip of it, or will you drive as efficiently as possible, with you and your passenger taking eight-hour shifts at the wheel, stopping only for gas and coffee?

The same goes for knowing how you'll be hired. Whether the church wants to or has to call a new pastor, they'll have to go through a search process.[4] I often find that candidates, even those in the latter stages of a job search, don't fully understand what steps a church must complete to make the hire. This confusion manifests itself when someone—a spouse or friend or family member—asks how close you are to being hired. The response goes something like, "You know, I'm not sure. The church said something about an interview weekend, but also something about a theology examination and calling references. But I don't know exactly when and how all of this happens."

Get It in Writing

This confusion over the specifics of the process is often multiplied when someone offers a job unsolicited. Maybe the person is a friend, or they are a member of a church you have prior experience with, or maybe you have no context for them at all but, for one reason or another, they know about you and want you to work for them.

If someone approaches you unsolicited and asks if you'd work for them, the first thing you should do is ask them to put the job description in writing if you're at all interested. It's possible they reached out to you on impulse with an opportunity that will never materialize. If they do produce a written job description, ask them what the hiring process will look like. If they don't know, they're not ready to hire you.

Also related to the unsolicited job offer, it's not uncommon for a volunteer ministry position to become a part-time or even a full-time

---

[4] It's better to refer to the hiring of a pastor as "calling a pastor" because of what the term communicates. In this book, however, I am using "hire" and "call" interchangeably.

position. As a church grows or restructures, often a key volunteer leader can be conscripted into a more official capacity. This can be a wonderful thing, but I'd encourage you to follow the same advice: get the offer in writing and treat the interview process as you would if you were an outside candidate. Many a volunteer-youth-pastor-turned-fulltime-youth-pastor has been mistreated by his employer because neither church nor employee came to a shared and realistic understanding of the job description, compensation, and authority structure.

Church Polity Hiring Considerations

Some confusion about the church hiring process is understandable. Unlike Starbucks or The Home Depot, Christian churches have no standardized process for hiring. It varies widely from one church to another. This variation is owing to a number of factors, especially church polity. Will you ultimately be hired by the senior pastor, the elder board, the congregation, or a denominational overseer such as a bishop? These questions of authority, appointment, and ability to make hiring decisions are important.

You might know this already, so this may just be a quick refresher, but there are three main types of church government.[5]

First, there's Episcopal polity. In Episcopal government (Catholic, Orthodox, Lutheran Church–Missouri Synod, Anglican, and Episcopal), pastors are appointed by denominational overseers. That's what the word *episkopos* means—an overseer or bishop (cf., 1 Tim 3:1). Because of this hierarchical structure, pastoral searches (at least at the senior level) aren't typically conducted because there's no need. The denomination assigns pastors to churches, and that's that.

Second, there's Presbyterian polity. Presbyterian churches are elder ruled, which means the elders are the final authority for decisions in the church. This doesn't mean, however, that you as a candidate will necessarily interact with the elder board during the hiring process. A presbyterian, elder-ruled church might commission a dedicated

---

[5] Some of these details about polity were adapted from William Vanderbloemen, *Search: The Pastoral Search Committee Handbook* (Nashville: B&H, 2016), 32–34.

search team to complete most, or perhaps all, of the search and hire. A variation of this government is a staff-led church, where the staff—or some senior portion thereof—functions as an elder board. This frequently occurs in nondenominational churches, especially large ones.

The other main type of polity is congregational. In congregational government (Baptist churches, Evangelical Free Churches, and many nondenominational churches), the congregation creates its own structure through its bylaws and constitution. The authority in these congregational churches principally rests, as you might expect, with the congregation.

However, many congregational churches delegate some authority to elders to lead and make decisions. The elders in a congregational government may or may not have the final authority to hire someone. It all depends. More than likely, if you're a senior pastor, you can expect a church vote will be required to officially hire you. What percentage of congregational approval constitutes a passing vote—66, 75, or 90 percent? It all depends. If you're not interviewing for a senior pastorate, it's hard to predict if a vote will be required, but likely it will not.

Other Hiring Considerations

Church polity isn't the only determining factor in the hiring process. It's likely that two Presbyterian churches that are otherwise equal in every major way will have vastly different steps in their own hiring processes. For example, near the end of the process, the elders or the search committee might come to visit you on your home turf. Or they might fly you to visit them in their context. They might do this once, or they might do it several times.

When will your spouse, if you're married, become involved? Will he or she be interviewed relatively early in the process (which is typically better for everyone involved) or very late in the process? If variations like these exist between two churches in the same denomination, it will certainly exist among nondenominational churches even more so.

Here's what I'm *not* saying. I'm not saying you should expect to experience job-search events that are unheard of, interviewing that is *sui generis*. Churches can only do so many things as they hire candidates. Nevertheless, processes vary. This variation can create understandable confusion for both candidates and churches. Churches, particularly smaller ones, don't get a lot of practice at hiring, and they don't particularly enjoy it when they do.

You have a few options if there seems to be significant confusion on the church's side of things. On the one hand, you could treat their confusion as a "red light": hit the brakes, come to a stop, and reevaluate. Near the end of the process, on the other hand, if the church seems to be confused about *what* they are supposed to be doing and *when* they are expected to be doing it, then this *might* be an opportunity for you as a candidate to lead them, a chance to begin pastoring them. I expect these cases are rare, but for the right pastor and the right church it just might be a wonderful opportunity. This is something you'll have to decide. Most of the time, however, confusion means it's time to walk away and start over with another church even if they're telling you to come. Set your flattered ego aside; you're not the savior of the church.

Speaking of flattery, never count on a position you're being promised until it's actually yours. If the head of a search team pulls you aside and says, "You're our number one candidate," take it with a grain of salt. If the former pastor says you're a shoo-in as his replacement, don't believe it. One seasoned pastor told me, "I have had positions taken away from me after being promised, 'We will take you from darkness to light; we will care for your family; we will pay you what you deserve.' I've heard it all. Most of the churches that made me the big promises, they never came to fruition." During one search that was down to the final two candidates, another pastor told me, "The chairman of the elders was taking me to the airport at the end of the weekend, and he was like, 'Hey, we're really interested; we're going to call you [as pastor]; we really enjoyed this.' And then he said, something along the lines of, 'We're going to bring in the other guy next weekend because we already told him that we would, but we're going to call you.'" But they didn't hire him. They hired the other guy.

Steps to Call a Pastor

Let's get more concrete. In broad terms, the following is what one hiring process might look like. Some of the steps may occur in a slightly different order in your situation, such as the timing of when a church calls a candidate's references and when you negotiate salary. Additionally, other steps may be skipped altogether, such as the optional steps early in the process or the video conference interview (especially if the candidate is local).

Preliminary steps of the hiring process

Step 1:	Former pastor announces resignation (or is terminated) and transition process begins.
Step 2:	[Optional] Leadership conducts an exit interview with the outgoing pastor.
Step 3:	[Optional] Leadership (and congregation) evaluates the need for an interim pastor and acts accordingly.
Step 4:	[Optional] Leadership conducts a congregational survey.
Step 5:	Search team is assembled and begins to meet.[6]
Step 6:	[Optional] Search team and leadership have meetings with denominational representatives and other consultants.
Step 7:	Search team and leadership create an official job description and compensation package. They also create, whether formally or informally, the profile of their "ideal" pastor (age, experience, education, skillset, theological and philosophical DNA, etc.).[7]
Step 8:	Possible internal candidates are considered or are asked to participate in the public process.

---

[6] Church polity will determine the exact process of how the team is formed, whether by the unilateral appointment of church leadership or by receiving nominations and a congregational vote.

[7] The profile of their ideal candidate will of course be within an internal document, something not shared with you.

Public steps of the hiring process

Step 9:   Position advertised publicly.

Step 10:   Resumes are received.

Step 11:   Candidates complete a pastoral information packet.

Step 12:   Phone interviews (possibly several of them).

Step 13:   Request for (more) sermon samples (or worship videos, etc.).

Step 14:   References are contacted.

Step 15:   Video conference interview (possibly several of them, with one including spouse).

Step 16:   Background check completed.

Step 17:   In-person interviews, but not over a weekend.

Step 18:   Potential hiring details are negotiated, including start date and salary package.

Step 19:   Candidating weekend (maybe longer than a weekend and will likely include many formal and informal interviews, possibly a sermon, a congregational Q&A, and a vote).

Step 20:   Hiring details are re-negotiated.

Step 21:   Church issues a formal call for candidate to pastor their church.

Step 22:   Candidate accepts formal call.

Step 23:   Church sends official letter of hire outlining terms of employment.

Step 24:   Installation of new pastor.

Twenty-four steps! That's a lot of steps, right? It sure is, but again, not every search will involve each step. Still, in the best churches the process will always be long and involved. Chris Brauns writes, "The number of interviews will depend on factors that vary from church to church. In my experience, it would not be unusual to have more than fifteen hours of interviews [with the candidate who ultimately gets the job]."[8] This estimation likely only includes the formal interviews; if all

---

[8] Brauns, *When the Word Leads Your Pastoral Search*, 146.

the informal social interactions are included, especially from across the candidating weekend, the total hours would be far higher.

Simply put, don't shy away from asking questions about how you'll be hired. Knowing what's coming next will help you prepare for the individual steps as they unfold. Is the next interview a theological one? Great, you'll be ready. Is it an informal discussion with your spouse where they'll ask to hear his or her testimony? Great, prepare for that one too.

Knowing the process and what's coming next will also help you prepare emotionally. It will be deflating to think you've reached the end of the road only to find out there's more to be done. After four straight days in the car on your road trip to LA, you don't want to confuse crossing Arizona's border with California's; you still have ten hours to go.

* * *

"Listening to the Spoken and the Unspoken"

By Cara Croft

Our son was four, our daughter was two, one of them had strep throat, and I was newly pregnant with our third child, which equaled nausea and fatigue.

This was the setting for the potluck that the church was hosting to get to know our family. It was not set up to be a formal interview; it was called an "introduction" or something along those lines. However, it was by all means an interview. Questions were asked to my husband, and the stories and failures of past pastors and their wives were all retold to me. For my husband, the pressure and examination were direct. For me and my children, however, it was indirect, even subtle. So subtle, in fact, that I did not realize at the time what was happening. I thought they were simply sharing the stories of their church. A few months after starting at the church, I began to realize the importance of what those members had shared when I was failing to meet the expectations I was promised did not exist.

"The pastor's wife did not even come to the church service"

translated into "so be sure to never miss a service—*ever*." "I have run Vacation Bible School for twenty years" meant "so be prepared to take it over because I am done." "Our Women's Ministry Union meets on Tuesdays at 1:00" was the spoken. "So when are you going to come to a meeting and lead this too?" was the unspoken. "We have not had a baby in the nursery in ten years" is what they said as they looked at my two children, and "Do not expect us to watch yours" was left unsaid when they found out I was pregnant with my third. It did not take long, however, for the unspoken to become spoken. Their disappointment at my inabilities showed quickly.

I don't share these things to discourage you. Ministry has been encouraging, but it has also been tough. As hard as we try, we will never know everything we need to know before stepping into a job. Never. No matter how many questions we ask.

If you were sitting with me at my favorite coffee shop right now, this is what I would tell you: Pay attention to the spoken and the unspoken stories. You are stepping into a church that has likely been wounded by its previous pastor and his wife. You will be expected to heal those wounds and not cause any more, but you will fail to do both. We fail because we rush to try to do what only God can do in his timing.

Stories are a language we all use to share what's beneath the surface, so listen to them. People are trying to share the ways they have been hurt, the ways they have felt loved, the ways they are tired of serving, the ways they love to serve, and the things that make them feel secure or threatened. Their stories tell you what they desire from you. Does this mean you and your family have to meet their standards? Absolutely not! But listening and paying attention will help you understand these sheep more accurately. And understanding them more accurately will, in turn, help you to love them more deeply.

Cara Croft is the director of Women's Ministry for Practical Shepherding and coauthor of the book *The Pastor's Family: Shepherding Your Family Through the Challenges of Pastoral Ministry*. Cara is wife to pastor and author Brian Croft, a mother of four, and a current student working on a master's degree in Christian counseling.

OVER-PREPARE FOR INTERVIEWS

*I worked harder . . . though it was not I, but
the grace of God that is with me.*
– 1 Corinthians 15:10

However much time you think you need to prepare for a job interview, double it. I don't say this because you need more busywork. Preparing for job interviews isn't busy work; it's mission critical.

As a candidate, you need to make sure you're truly prepared for interviews, and to become *truly* prepared, I advocate being over-prepared. If you feel over-prepared, you've probably adequately prepared.

I learned this principle as a young engineer. At the construction company where I worked, we billed every hour of design directly to a project. For my first year or two, this led me to feel tremendous pressure to complete my jobs as quickly as possible.

When it came time for installation, however, let's just say the union construction workers were pretty good at letting me know I hadn't done my homework, even suggesting the paper my installation plans were printed on should be used for a more ignoble purpose. Not only was this humbling, but it was also a poor use of company money. It didn't help the bottom line for me to "save" one hour only to have ten people stand around for that same one hour while they fixed my mistake. This happened often enough that I finally began to "over-engineer," as I called it, all my designs.

And what was the result? Adequate engineering.

So, to get to this place of adequate readiness, focus on over-preparing in these areas.

Over-Prepare to Know the Particular Dynamics of Your Interview Type

The first thing you need to know is what kind of interview you're about to experience and its potential pitfalls. Here are some of the typical types of interviews for prospective pastors:

1. Paper application with short-answer essays;
2. Telephone interview with one person;
3. Telephone interview with *more* than one person;
4. Video-conference interview with one person;
5. Video-conference interview with *more* than one person;
6. In-person interview one-on-one;
7. In-person interview with a group;
8. Candidating weekend.

You'll likely experience all eight of these types of interviews—some of them more than once—if you continue through the interview process to its completion. It will benefit you to think through and prepare for what issues might arise with each of these.

For example, with a phone interview, you might receive a call that surprises you, so plan beforehand to ask if you can call them back in thirty minutes or whatever time makes sense. This extra time will prove valuable, especially if you are pursuing several jobs simultaneously; you'll want a chance to refresh your memory to make sure you're keeping them straight. Typically, requesting to call them back won't be an issue to the potential employer, but if you haven't planned for this scenario, you'll likely just take the call when it comes and stumble through it on the fly. One pastor, because he recognized the number and desperately didn't want to miss the call, answered his phone just seconds after finishing a jog. In hindsight, he wished he had waited to catch his breath and talked to the church when he wasn't still wheezing.

Video conference interviews (i.e., Skype, Google Hangouts, Zoom, FaceTime) can also present challenges. For example, expect slight delays due to poor Internet connection. From experience, I can say these delays often cause people to interrupt each other unintentionally. "You go first—" "No, no, you go—" "Okay, okay, I'll start . . ." Also know these delays often make attempts at humor difficult.[1] Over-preparing will help you overcome these challenges.

In the interview process you need to lay your theological cards on the table, but in the early phases don't be so zealous with secondary doctrines. It was a huge red flag when one young pastor gushed his Reformed convictions in the first two minutes of an interview. When you do that, it sets the search team on edge because they might think this is how you'll interact in your initial conversations with every person in their congregation, even if that's not the case.

If the candidate lives close enough for search committee members to drive out for a visit (and sometimes even if he or she does not), members from the team may visit the candidate's home church. This is often helpful, but it creates challenges too. One of them is how to structure the visit so that the search team does not stand out. This is more difficult at a small church, though there are ways to make it easier. You might try asking team members to come to different services (if there are multiple services) or at least to enter at different times and sit in different parts of the sanctuary. This might seem silly, like you're hosting foreign spies, but if confidentiality is crucial, they must be discreet.

---

[1] Just one more piece of advice related to video conferences: as much as possible, look at the camera, not the screen. If you don't look at the camera, it will seem as though you're not looking them in the eyes, which is true, though it's not on purpose. If you find it too hard to look at the camera the entire time, at least try to do it at strategic moments, such as saying hello, asking your questions, talking about something personal, and as you finish the interview. Over-preparing on video conferences may include practicing with a friend.

Finally, never forget while you are around people—whether at their church or yours—that both you and your spouse are being watched. If the senior pastor and his family take you to an ice cream shop after a long day of interviewing, don't let your guard down. You're still interviewing.

Over-Prepare to Make Your Interview Answers Short

If you're like most people, you tend to ramble when you're not adequately prepared. Your answers aren't crisp and clean. This isn't good for interviewing. It makes you look indecisive, like you're guessing. Rarely does anyone improve their answers through length (whether on written applications or in oral interviews).

Besides looking indecisive, long answers don't help for another reason—perhaps a surprising one. Those who are asking the questions in interviews are often *more* interested in asking their next question than they are in listening to you drone on and on about the current question. This is particularly the case in group interviews when people take turns asking questions. It's selfish, I know, and it's a reflection of our hearts, but it's just how it is. So remember, shorter is better.

Additionally, realize that an interview is a time for you to be examined, not to teach. The search team is there to find out what you believe, how strongly you believe it, and how well you can articulate it. They already know (or *should* know) what their church believes about the end times and spiritual gifts and homosexuality and the age of the earth. You're not there to teach them. If you try, it will seem out of place at best and arrogant at worst.

Finally, know the difference between authenticity and disclosing every single sin. This requires discernment. "Millennials aren't very good at this," one executive pastor told me. "They tend to think honesty and authenticity are the same as verbal diarrhea." The church doesn't need to know *everything* about you. You don't need to pour your heart out along with all its emotions. What they need to know are the honest facts about your life that would be helpful to them in making the decision about hiring you. People sometimes mistakenly share things in an interview not reflective of who they are in the Lord right now.

Over-Prepare to Nail the Expected Interview Questions

When you know that something about you will likely generate questions from the employer, make sure you're ready for it.

These can be neutral things. For instance, if you're accustomed to living in Southern California and the potential job is in Maine, the search committee will want to know if you really know what four months of heavy snow is like. Maybe you lived in Maine as a child and are excited to get back or maybe you have no idea what it will be like, but before they ask, anticipate the question and prepare a response.

Some things, on the other hand, might generate questions that are less than neutral. For example, did you resign or were you fired from your last job?

Here are some other questions for you to prepare for: Have you been previously married? Has your spouse? Are you currently in a liberal denomination (or seminary) but looking for employment in a conservative church—or vice versa? Did your church experience a split, or maybe just a splinter, during your pastorate? Are you unable to move for six months because of a contractual agreement with your current employer? Have you been out of work for some time? Have you been charged with drunk driving? Are you far younger or older than other people applying or not as formally educated? Was much of your ministry experience in a parachurch organization?

If any one of these apply to you, or a hundred other possibilities only you know, then prepare; have your answers ready. Most concerns can be resolved with a good explanation—and if there isn't one, then say so. The gospel teaches us we are sinners saved by grace. This allows us to take ownership of our past because our past doesn't define us—Christ does. Also, if there are questions that can be better answered by someone else, mention this too. For example, if there was a church split under your leadership or you were let go from your church, it will be valuable to have references who know the inside details of the situation and who will vouch for how you conducted yourself. If others are at fault, it most likely will come across better from your references than from you.

Over-Prepare to End the Interview Well

Certainly you should end the meeting by thanking people for their time, but beyond this, you may have questions for them you don't want to forget. You want to know when you might expect to hear back from them or when they expect the new hire to begin employment.

It sounds silly, but if you haven't prepared for how you'll end the interview, you might just keep talking and talking and talking. I've seen it happen. People get excited and just keep going. Don't be that person. You don't want to end the interview rambling about this or that, telling an anecdote about your new puppy or your new car or maybe about how you were recently injured while training for a half-marathon—which by the way was your first half-marathon—but this injury isn't gonna stop you from being a great new hire and preaching great sermons, that's for sure, because you'll be ready for that, just like the time when . . .

Meanwhile, everyone else in the interview will be thinking to themselves, *I wish he knew when to stop.*

Learn Names to Make a Personal Connection

People say I'm naturally gifted at learning names. To some extent that might be true. The full truth, however, is that I cheat.

But before I tell you *how* I cheat, let me stress *why*, as a pastor, I labor to learn the names of those who attend our church and the leaders of a potential church during the hiring process.

Why Knowing Names Matters

We should learn names for at least two reasons. First, a general reason: God has always existed in relationship—the loving relationship of Father, Son, and Spirit. And because we're made in God's image and likeness, it's not good for us to be alone. I believe this is the main reason why people desire to be where everyone knows their name, just like the tagline from *Cheers.* God designed us for community.

But more than our general longing to be known, there's also a specific reason why I want to excel at learning the names of my congregants. Embedded within the universal longing to be known, there seem to be echoes of the specific longing for relationship with God. We want the shepherd of a church to know the names of his sheep, just as the Good Shepherd knows the names of all his sheep (John 10:14).

Many people in the Bible are nameless to us, but God knows their names. From the Israelites who were set free from Egypt, to the 7,000 who hadn't bowed the knee to Baal, to the 5,000 who ate the two fish and five loaves, to the 3,000 who were added to the church at Pentecost, to the countless multitude in Revelation—none are nameless to him. The Great Shepherd knows all of them by name.

God's knowledge of his people is intimate and particular. When the Bible says Jesus knows the names of his sheep, it's a figure of speech revealing a deeper truth. Just as "lend me a hand" and "boots on the ground" are about more than hands and boots, so it is with knowing names. Jesus lovingly knows his sheep's birthdays and anniversaries, their passions and longings, their wounds and fears, their sins and failures, the hairs on their heads and the length of their days.

We'll never know all these intricacies about others nor even about ourselves. Nevertheless, Jesus's shepherding creates the paradigm for ours. What Jesus does perfectly, we strive to approximate as we "shepherd the flock of God that is among [us]" (1 Pet 5:2). Following this pattern means we must know the sheep he has put in our charge—starting with, and certainly moving beyond, simply knowing their names.

Tips for Learning Names

Learning names is a skill we can improve with practice. I do several things to improve.

With my last two ministry transitions, the process of learning names began during the interview stage. I'd scour the church's website and Facebook page looking for people in leadership. I also asked for access to their church picture directory (if they had one). Then, I'd make flash cards and study like I was cramming for a Hebrew exam.

Perhaps this sounds excessive, but it makes a huge difference. Once, when introduced to eight leaders in a group interview, they made the obligatory quip, "You probably won't remember our names." Yet over the next two hours I was able to speak to each person by name.

If this method isn't for you, two more require less homework. First, when you end a conversation with someone new, ask, "Could you remind me of your name again?" This is socially acceptable because no one begrudges this the first time you meet, maybe even the second. It's often in restating the name that I catch it, especially if I repeat the name by saying something like, "I really enjoyed meeting you, Joe."

Also, ask people to restate their names each time they contribute during a Sunday school class or Bible study. People probably won't remember to do this, so you'll have to remind them a few times. If it's a lengthy meeting, however, don't make them continue doing it the whole time. If you do, it will come across as rude and forgetful, thereby undermining the whole point.

Like most churches, mine has a transient fringe, those people who are neither members nor regular attendees. I'll probably never learn their names; indeed, they haven't given me a chance. And if this is true in my smaller church, it's that much more difficult for the lead pastor to know everyone's name in a larger one. Still, we should make an effort to know more names than we do. Putting in this unseen effort to learn people's names goes a long way in showing you really care.

Be advised, though, that learning names requires bravery; you have to be willing to look foolish. As our church has grown in the last few years, it's been more difficult to keep names straight. Recently, I called one woman Jennifer, which wasn't her name, as she gently reminded me. Swing and a miss. But I've gotten her name right ever since.

Have a Mock Interview

A mock interview is another way to over-prepare, and it proved to be one of the most helpful—and least enjoyable—things I did during my own job search.

When I was looking for my first pastoral job, I'd participated in interviews many times but never in the context of a local church. All my experience had been in the business world. To be sure, there's some significant overlap, but when I interviewed with engineering firms, no one ever asked me to articulate the gospel, explain the Trinity, tell them whether all the small groups in a church should use the same curriculum or choose their own, or what spiritual gifts my wife has. They didn't ask these kinds of questions, so I needed practice at answering them.

One of the elders at my local church wisely offered to create a mock interview for me. He recruited several other mature Christians at our church, and they grilled me for about two hours on a Tuesday night in a classroom at our church. Then, they gave me feedback for another hour.

It was miserable.

But why? Were they mean? Not at all. Were they unfair? Nope.

It was miserable because I thought I was good at interviewing, but as it turned out, I wasn't. The experience was deeply humbling, maybe even humiliating. Invariably, my answers were too long and unrelated to the actual question. I had a lot to learn. Likely, so do you.

Before you begin the interviewing phase of a job search, schedule a mock interview. The best people to conduct one are those in your church who have sat on search committees before or those who have hiring responsibilities in their own job. If you don't have this, recruit some friends to do this for you.

Potential Questions for a Mock Interview

To conduct a mock interview you need to know the right questions to ask. To alleviate this burden, I've compiled a list of questions you can use as a starting point. If you need more, you could easily expand upon the questions by doing an Internet search[2] or by consulting the

---

[2] For example, "What Kind of Questions Should a Church Ask a Pastoral Candidate?" *9Marks*, https://www.9marks.org/answer/what-kind-questions-should-church-ask-pastoral-candidate/.

extensive lists in *Moving On—Moving Forward* and *From M.Div. to Rev.*[3]

Before I turn you loose, let me point out a few things. Most of the questions below fall into the category of behavioral interview questions. This is intentional. Behavioral questions focus on what a candidate has done, not what he or she might do in some hypothetical scenario. For example, one question might be, "Tell us about a time in ministry when you *were* in conflict with a person and how you resolved it," as opposed to, "If someone didn't like one of your new ministry initiatives, tell us how you *might* respond to them." Another could be, "How *have* you chosen which passages to preach?" not, "How *might* you choose what passages to preach?"

If the search team asks you hypothetical questions, do your best to ground your responses in concrete examples. What you've done in the past and how you've learned from it is by far a better predictor of what you'll do in the future than your theoretical pontifications. Wouldn't you rather know if a football coach *did* go for the end zone on a fourth and goal with twenty seconds left when he was down by three, rather than what he *might* do if such a situation ever arose? I sure would.

I've also noticed that the legacy of the former pastor tends to lurk behind interview questions. The more obscure the question, the more likely there's a backstory. When questions bore in about your preaching style, worship song selection, method for disciplining your own children, whether you'll have a candlelight service on Christmas Eve, or how you'd handle a marital affair by someone in leadership, the deeper question might very well be, *Are you like our previous pastor?* The hoped-for answer might be yes or it might be no. But if you sense a question-behind-the-question, don't keep elaborating and justifying your position. Pause. Then ask, "How has that been done here in the past?"

---

[3] Michael J. Anthony and Mick Boersma, *Moving On—Moving Forward: A Guide for Pastors in Transition* (Grand Rapids, MI: Zondervan, 2007), 230–31, and Eubanks, *From M.Div. to Rev.*, 199–208.

Interview Practice Questions

Personal, Family, and Hobbies

1. Tell us about how you became a Christian.
2. Tell us about your daily walk with God and your call to ministry.
3. Do you now struggle with pornography or have you in the past? What steps do you have in place to fight against this common temptation?
4. What are you reading these days? Who are some of your favorite authors and speakers?
5. What movies and books have you enjoyed recently?
6. Do you describe yourself as an introvert or extrovert? Why?
7. What do you like to do in your free time? Do you play any instruments? Do you have a favorite sport to play or watch?
8. If you are married, how did you meet your spouse? Tell us about your children (if you have them).
9. In the last week, what have you done to show your spouse he or she is the most important person in your life?
10. How have you balanced church demands with other responsibilities, especially the needs of your family?
11. How does your family feel about the potential move?
12. What do family devotions look like in your home?
13. Outside of church ministry, do you have other ministry commitments, such as speaking at camps, writing projects, adjunct teaching, chaplaincy, music bands, etc.?
14. How is your current financial situation, including your personal debt level?

Experience and Job Description

15. What were your favorite and least favorite classes in seminary? Why?
16. Why are you leaving your current ministry role?
17. Why are you interested in this job? Do you see yourself doing it for several years?

18. What are your greatest strengths? Weaknesses?[4]

19. How do you structure your typical workweek in ministry?

20. What excites you about this job?

21. Are you considering getting more formal education?

22. What aspect(s) of this ministry do you feel least qualified for and why?

23. Which aspect of the job description or this church gives you the most concern?

24. Tell me about a time when something went very wrong in ministry. What did you learn?

25. Describe a time when a church you were at went through a season of great change. In what ways did the leadership handle it well? In what ways did they handle it poorly?

26. Tell us about your experience overseeing staff and volunteers. Do you enjoy this?

27. Which style of worship service do you feel most comfortable in (e.g., contemporary, traditional, blended, liturgical)?

28. What is your experience with older members of the church?

29. Have you officiated memorial and funeral services? Can you tell us about a particularly meaningful memorial service you led?

30. Tell us about some of the unchurched people you have invited to your church and interacted with in the last six months.

31. [For music leaders] How do you go about choosing music sets for church worship? To what extent do you try to work with the preaching pastor on this?

32. [For youth leaders] List these in order of importance to the success or your ministry: elders, parents, volunteer leaders, students. Why?

33. [For youth leaders] To what extent do you involve parents in youth group and why?

---

[4] It's become cliché to ask these two questions, but alas, I list them anyway because you'll likely be asked. If you are asked, do not answer the question about weaknesses with positive sounding "flaws." If you do, you'll sound like Michael Scott from the television show *The Office*. In one episode, Michael was asked during a job interview, "What do you think are your greatest strengths as a manager?" To this Michael answered, "Why don't I tell you what my greatest weaknesses are? I work too hard. I care too much. And sometimes I can be too invested in my job." Please don't be like Michael Scott ("The Job," *The Office*, season 3, episode 23, NBC, May 17, 2007).

Pastoral

34. How would you describe your preaching style?
35. Describe the process you use to prepare a sermon. How long do you typically spend preparing a sermon?
36. How do you choose which passages to preach?
37. What are some of your favorite sermons and why?
38. Do you have any pet peeves about church websites and church worship services? What are they and why?
39. Of the spiritual gifts noted in Scripture, what are yours? How have you seen these spiritual gifts affirmed?
40. What has been your personal practice regarding tithing? How does your church giving relate to your other giving (e.g., parachurch organizations)?
41. What aspects make for a healthy church?
42. How important are small groups in a local church? Of the different groups you have participated in, describe what made them healthy or unhealthy.
43. Tell us about a few of the discipling relationships you have been in, one with you primarily discipling and one with you primarily being discipled.
44. How do you feel about church administration? What role has it played in your previous jobs?
45. Name a doctrine you hold that you consider to be of secondary importance. How have you taught about it publicly?
46. Should the Sunday morning service be directed mainly to believers or unbelievers? Do you prepare so it can speak to both audiences?
47. How have you maintained the balance between cultural relevance and faithfulness in gospel ministry? Or is this something that can't be, or shouldn't be, balanced?
48. Tell us about a time you had to practice church discipline. What is the motivation for church discipline?
49. What are the more important issues facing our denomination?

Theological

50. Describe the last gospel conversation you had with a non-Christian.
51. Where do you see evidence of the Trinity in Scripture?
52. Would any important doctrines be compromised if the virgin birth was denied?
53. Do you believe you should include the gospel every time you preach or teach? What would it mean to do this well and what would it mean to do it poorly? How have you included, or not included, the gospel when preaching from an Old Testament passage?
54. Define justification, conversion, repentance, election, perseverance, and regeneration.
55. Describe the relationship, if you think there is one, between conversion, baptism, church membership, and the Lord's Supper.
56. What theological positions do you hold that might be considered controversial?
57. Which, if any, of your theological views have changed in the last five years? Why?
58. It seems like many children who grow up in the church leave the church when they leave home. In your understanding, what are some of the reasons for this?
59. How do you understand the terms *inerrant* and *infallible*?
60. As you have looked at our statement of faith, what questions do you have about it? Will you be able to teach in accordance with it? Do you take exception with any point?

Controversial Topics

61. What is your view of men's and women's roles within the home and the church?
62. What is your view of the end times?
63. What is your view of the days of creation?
64. What are your views on the gifts of tongues, prophecy, and healing?

65. What is your view of the relationship between God's sovereignty and human responsibility, specifically in salvation?
66. What is your view on Christians and alcohol consumption? Do you personally drink alcohol?
67. What is your view of abortion and euthanasia? How have you counseled someone who was having struggles regarding the beginning or the end of life (e.g., someone with an unplanned pregnancy or someone with a loved one on life support)?
68. What is your view of divorce and remarriage? Have you ever told a couple you would not officiate their wedding? If so, why?
69. How should the church approach homosexuality and issues of gender?

Questions for a Candidate's Spouse

70. What do you enjoy doing with your free time?
71. What has your career looked like over the years?
72. How did you meet your spouse?
73. How did you become a Christian?
74. How do you and your spouse decide who does what in your home?
75. What was your family like growing up?
76. Do you plan to work outside the home?
77. What schooling choice have you and your spouse made for your children?
78. How do you feel about taking this job and moving?
79. What do you feel is your role as a pastor's spouse?
80. How do you hope to be involved at our church?
81. What qualities do you appreciate about your spouse?
82. What could we do for you to help make this process as meaningful but also as painless as possible?
83. What questions do you have for us?

Debrief After an Interview

Be certain to debrief your mock interview shortly after it's completed, if not right away. If you don't, valuable feedback will slip away. Again, it's better to be humbled in a fake interview than a real one.

You should also ask for feedback after official interviews, even from churches who *didn't* give you the job. If you do ask this from a church, be sure to allay any fears this is a ploy to try to get the job even though they already told you no. Make sure they know this is just your desire to learn.

I remember one phone interview that I could tell wasn't going well. (Yes, I had several of these.) It was no surprise when I found out I wouldn't be continuing to the next round. The pastor and elder who interviewed me seemed like nice, thoughtful men, so I asked the pastor if he'd be willing to give me some feedback. Jackpot. The phone call to debrief was twice the length of my interview! Not only did he tell me things I could improve on but, because he'd just finished a long stretch of interviews, I also heard all the other helpful (and unhelpful) things other candidates did.

Asking for this kind of direct feedback helps because on the first pass churches often won't tell you the real reasons why they are rejecting you. One pastor told me, "When they do tell you, they lie. They don't want to hurt you. They won't tell you they don't like your theology, don't think you are capable of preaching to a large audience, or found your mannerisms annoying." This, in my experience, is a bit like when church members leave. It's hard to know the real reasons, and even when you do have something like an exit interview, only rarely do you get the truth unless you really dig for it. But when you do, the information you gain is worth the effort.

Just like networking, interviewing can be a rough experience, but it doesn't have to be. If you understand the process and you've prepared accordingly, it can be a wonderful time to articulate your gifts, theological convictions, and philosophy of ministry. And it can be a time where—in a very real sense—God speaks to you and guides you to the place he's calling you to serve.

* * *

"Wear Your Beliefs on Your Sleeve"

By J. A. Medders

The Home Depot and I don't belong together. I'm a foreigner in this strange store. It's a playground for men and women who know what to do with tools, electricity, plumbing, and other home-related who-sie-whatsits. When I pretend like I know what I'm doing, and I tackle a DIY project at my house, I always regret it. From putting holes in the wall when I was just unscrewing a towel rack to electricity bolting through my body, I'm no handyman. I'm not wired for it. I've come to terms with who I am, and my house and sanity are better for it.

One of the worst things you could do as you interview to become a church's pastor is to gloss over certain theological stances you have because it might keep you from getting the job. Don't hide who you are. Doctrinal deception is disqualifying. If you begin your ministry with deceit, you've already derailed it. Don't let the pursuit of a pastorate push your beliefs to the background. If this temptation lurks in the interview, know that an unhealthy pursuit for ministry is behind it all. Ministry idolatry will help you get a ministry—and then it'll help you ruin it. One way you can crucify this idolatry, or fear, is by owning your convictions. Make them known, and let the job offers fall where they may.

Show the committee, the elders, or whoever is interviewing you that you take the Bible seriously and you have given credible, pastoral thought to a variety of doctrines that matter in discipleship with the risen Jesus. Doctrine is for discipleship. Theology is never irrelevant. It matters for sermons, counseling, staff meetings, search committees, job offers, and every situation under the sun.

If you are a Calvinist, don't hide your TULIP because its aroma might offend. Talk about the bouquet of God's grace in a gracious manner. If you pray in tongues, let them know. Maybe the church will encourage it, or maybe they will end the interview right then. Whatever the outcome, own your views. If you believe in a rapture, don't leave that behind. Does your position on the end times differ from the church's?

As you do your homework on this local church, itemize potential places of disagreement, grade how critical the disagreement is to you, and then have this conversation in the process. How flexible are you on the frequency of communion? Where do you and the church land on baptism? Credo, paedo, a hybrid? Does the church's structure and practice for eldership and deacons align with yours? Make your list, see where there can be unity in diversity or if there's too much disagreement—on either side—to serve effectively. Do it for your benefit and the church's.

It's better to talk about controversial theological issues in an interview than in a conflict resolution meeting or a meeting where the church is voting to fire you. You don't want to turn a blind eye to any theological positions or church practices, because it will eventually come back around. Your secret stances will become obvious. The tension will snowball. The drama will escalate and then a new secret search committee will accept their mission. You can save yourself the time of moving your family and attending many tense meetings if you'll simply say what you believe.

As you unfold your personal views, see where the church may be open to change and where there are thick walls of concrete. When a pastor differs too much from the doctrinal distinctives of a church, it's best to pack up, thank everyone for their time, and move along. If they are open to your views or open to being convinced from God's word about fill-in-the-blank, keep the conversation going. Be who you are. Show what you believe. Don't act like me, a hypocrite in The Home Depot.

J. A. Medders is Lead Pastor of Redeemer Church, Tomball, Texas. He's the author of *Humble Calvinism* and *Rooted* and is a blogger and speaker as well as the host of the *Home Row* podcast for writers.

EVALUATE THE TRANSPLANT CRITERIA

For everything there is a season, and a time for every matter under heaven . . . a time to plant, and a time to pluck up what is planted.
– Ecclesiastes 3:1–2

"How much does it pay?" asks the would-be pastor during the interview.

This could be a good question, but if it's the *only* question the candidate is asking, then he's likely not called to a career in ministry.

Salary is important, and a generous salary might make a job desirable, but it's certainly not everything. Therefore, you must be evaluating *more* than salary; you should evaluate the complete fit. You can be sure a good church will be doing this with you.

Evaluate All the Pastoral Transplant Criteria

I have a few friends and family members in various stages of the organ-donation process. I've learned how seriously doctors take matching the right donor with the right person in need. They do this because the better the match, the higher the chance of a successful transplant.

Pastors can learn from this. When God calls us to move, we need to pay attention to the appropriate match criteria. If you're rash and don't consider the overall fit, it can end up hurting you, your family, *and* the church. In the most extreme cases, a pastor might even leave the ministry altogether, not because he wasn't suited or adequately trained for pastoral ministry but because the mismatch inflicted emotional, spiritual, and career-ending trauma.

Bo Lane, the founder of a ministry devoted to helping former pastors, underscores this importance: "Although there were many aspects of serving in full-time ministry that I loved, there were more things that happened along the way that made a negative impact on both myself and my family." Thankfully, Lane's ministry injuries weren't career ending, but his return wasn't necessarily quick. "After I resigned from the pastorate," he writes, "it took several years of forgiving and getting plugged in to a healthy church before I began to heal from the hurt."[1]

One pastor I know only lasted a year and a half in his first church. "It was partly my ignorance, not knowing what I was getting into. It really turned out to be a horrible fit." When he did leave that church, he thought about leaving ministry altogether: "It's one thing to tell a person that churches are tough and that some churches will chew you up and spit you out, but it is another thing to experience it, and especially for your spouse to experience it."

Similarly, Joel Rainey, writing to pastoral search teams, says this:

> Tragically, in my current role I've had a front row seat on too many occasions to witness pastors destroy churches, and I've also seen churches destroy pastors. What God clearly intended in Scripture to be a mutually beneficial relationship instead devolved into a caustic and spiritually abusive situation that brought personal hurt to the pastor and his family, gross

---

[1] Bo Lane, *Why Pastors Quit: Examining Why Pastors Quit and What We Can Do About It* (independently published, 2014), 15.

dysfunction to the congregation, and shame on the name of Jesus. *In a great number of these cases, the problem could have been avoided before the pastor was called to the church.*[2]

To help avoid this kind of trauma, let me briefly mention a few categories that can serve as significant indicators as to how well-matched a candidate is for a position. As one author writes, "Finding a job and finding the *right* job are two very different things."[3]

Evaluate Job Description

The first thing to consider is the job description. Ask questions like: Am I qualified to do this, in education and experience? Do I have a passion for it? Every job has aspects of grit-your-teeth duty, but could I be excited about doing this for forty to fifty hours a week, for fifty weeks a year, for the next five years—*or more*? Each local church is a unique manifestation of the bride of Christ and "must not be treated as a stepping-stone."[4]

If you look at enough job descriptions, you'll start to notice the descriptions themselves often fall into two categories: some being too big, in that expectations are unrealistic, and others being too small, in that expectations are unclear. Neither is necessarily wrong, but you should figure out which kind you're looking at and develop questions accordingly. It seems to me that it's more common for job descriptions to be too big. "So many churches," notes Mark Dever, "want twenty years of experience in a thirty-five-year-old pastor."[5]

Let me give you two examples, one too big and one too small. One job I interviewed for had a huge description associated with it. When I asked the church about this, I learned that in a year or two they hoped the job would be split in two, with a new pastor hired to do half the job. That's okay, I guess, but I'm glad I found this out beforehand so we could talk about which half of the job I'd (potentially) keep and which half I'd lose.

---

[2] Joel Rainey, *Side-Stepping Landmines: Five Principles for Pastor Search Teams* (Eldersburg, MD: Mid-Maryland Baptist Association, 2012), 4, emphasis added.

[3] Krueger, *The College Grad Job Hunter*, 1, emphasis added.

[4] Helopoulos, *The New Pastor's Handbook*, 36.

[5] Mark Dever, "Leadership | Session 1," September 29, 2017, https://www.9marks.org/message/leadership-mark-dever-session-1-9marks-at-southeastern-2017/.

In another interview, the job description was threadbare and ambiguous; I couldn't tell what the church expected this "Family Pastor" to do. So, I asked. They were still vague. So, I asked more specifically, "Take preaching, for example; there will only be two pastors on staff. Will the new pastor ever preach?" From the look on the senior pastor's face, not only did I know the answer was "no," but I also knew I had offended him by daring to ask. I, however, was glad I asked.

When you ask yourself if you're qualified to do this job, what should you do if the answer is "no"? You should move on, of course. Or maybe not. If the job description requires you to lead the music ministry but you can't play an instrument or hold a tune, then yes, spare yourself and everyone else and don't apply. If, however, the job description states that you must be able to officiate funerals and weddings, of which you have done little or none, then what do you do? If you like the church and your skills overlap with the rest of what's required, then consider pressing on. Maybe you tell the church, "I've never done X, Y, and Z, but I'll learn."

In short, don't shy away from applying just because you're not the "perfect" candidate; there won't be a perfect candidate. Churches craft job descriptions as a mixture of *must haves* and *wish list*. Whether your skills overlap well enough is a question for later in the process. Be aware, though, that the more jobs you apply for that are a half step, or even a full step, outside of your gifting and qualification sweet spot, the more you should expect to hear "Thanks but no thanks." When you shoot with a shotgun, don't expect every piece of buckshot to hit the target.

I'll say more about money in the next chapter, but related to job description I should probably make one comment now. Some churches will show a salary range and others will not. From a candidate's perspective, it would be wise for you to know something of the range before you get too deep in the process. This is a courtesy to all parties involved because time wasted on an untenable arrangement helps no one.

If no salary range is listed, they'll likely have a statement that says something to the effect of "compensation will be commensurate with education and experience." We should hope so, right? A statement like this, or none at all, shouldn't stop you from sending your cover letter and resume package, but it should be a talking point before you travel across the country for an onsite interview.

Evaluate Church Size and Surrounding Community

Another thing to consider is size—both the size of the church (and its association, if affiliated) and of the community. Keller writes,

> We tend to think of the chief differences between churches mainly in denominational or theological terms, but that underestimates the impact of size on how a church operates. The difference between how churches of 100 and 1,000 function may be much greater than the difference between a Presbyterian and a Baptist church of the same size. The staff person who goes from a church of 400 to a church of 2,000 is in many ways making a far greater change than if he or she moved from one denomination to another. A large church is not simply a bigger version of a small church. The difference in communication, community formation, and decision-making processes are so great that the leadership skills required in each are of almost completely different orders.[6]

As I was preparing to finish seminary and find a job, I wasn't sure I knew where my family and I would best fit, so to give us a better idea, we pursued a few different churches. Over time, there was one church that seemed like it could be a good fit. The onsite interview went well, the people were very friendly, and the gospel was clearly at work. Their community, however, was *very* rural. As my wife and I drove away from the interview, we realized we wouldn't be a good fit in a country church, even though many other things aligned quite well.

On the other end of the spectrum, I once interviewed at a thriving church in a college town. If hired, I would have been one of nine pastors on staff with an M.Div. This meant I would specialize in a ministry niche, which might have been great, but at the time I felt a broader role would be a better fit, both for them and for my future.

---

6 Timothy Keller, "Leadership and Church Size Dynamics: How Strategy Changes with Growth," *The Movement Newsletter*, 2006.

Every gospel-preaching church displays the glory of God—small and large, rural and urban, and everything in between. Nonetheless, not every church is right for you nor you for it. Work hard to find where God is specifically calling you.

Evaluate Theology

Be sure to evaluate theology. It matters what a church believes and how firmly (or loosely) they hold to those beliefs. You're probably equipped to assess this, but I bring it up to make sure you actually ask the questions necessary to discover a church's theological convictions. Don't make assumptions based on denominational affiliation or where the senior pastor received his degree.

Let's focus on denominations for a moment. Many people have the misunderstanding that, for example, a Baptist is a Baptist is a Baptist. But there are Independent Baptists, Free Will Baptists, Southern Baptists, Reformed Baptists, and many other types of Baptists. Even within the Southern Baptist denomination, which is the largest Protestant denomination in the world, there is considerable variation. A Baptist pastor might know the theological differences between them, but the typical parishioner does not. This means the typical search committee member may not know the differences between denominations either.

Only *after* taking up his new role as solo pastor, one rookie learned he was the only one in his church who actually believed his denomination's theology. The pushback he received after his hiring was inevitable, making it a rather difficult first year. In the end, it made for a turbulent and brief pastorate. "You get some churches on the fringe of a denomination," he said, "and you're not sure what they're doing. You make assumptions based on one elder [you get to know], and think, 'If that guy is there, then the whole church can't be that far off.'" But they can. Another pastor, after he'd already preached his candidating sermon in a church with Reformed soteriology, was asked by the head deacon, "What's this I hear about you believing in election?"

A similar thing almost happened to me. During an interview with one search team, as we were wrapping up, I was asked a question about my understanding of the relationship between God's sovereignty and human responsibility as it relates to the nature of salvation. Specifically, they wanted to know if I was an Arminian or a Calvinist. I gave my answer with conviction, but also (I hope) with appropriate humility. The search team nodded their heads as I explained, seemingly in approval.

When I finished speaking, the leader of the search team asked, "How do you think this will work out here, given our senior pastor has the opposite view?" At that moment it wasn't clear if his question was directed to the whole search team (as though they had never talked about this before), or if the question was only meant for me. If you want to know what happened next, I'll tell you: a long, awkward pause.

Both of us should have figured this out sooner.

Sometimes you can learn a church's theology from their statement of faith. At the very least, this will tell you their theology and core values as they exist on paper. But just as with people, actions sometimes betray actual beliefs. Be on the lookout for any serious disconnects. Author and professor Joseph Umidi advises his students in this way:

> Over the years, I have assigned some of my students the task of trying to discover a church's values without referring to any of its written documents. The project appears difficult until the students learn to switch their focus from what the church *says* about itself to what the church actually *does*. They begin to look at what the leaders are modeling in their lives as well as what they are preaching and teaching in their messages.... Ultimately, a church's budget (where they spend their money) and its programs (where they spend their time) make statements about the church's actual values, as opposed to those that are only *aspirational*.[7]

If helping the poor and evangelizing the lost show up on paper, look to see if there are ministries and resources dedicated to such things. You can also glean their theological moorings by asking

---

[7] Umidi, *Confirming the Pastoral Call*, 40, emphasis original.

questions about pastors and authors who are influencing the church and its leadership.

Evaluate Personality

Finally, evaluating fit means considering intangible and elusive things like personality. All churches, just like all people, have one. You'll need to discover it and find out if you can work naturally with one another.

In his book *What's Your Church's Personality?*, Philip Douglass identifies several areas where differing personalities bubble up. I've listed several to help you visualize the differences.

Achievement. How is effectiveness primarily defined? More people, growth of budget, expansion of church facilities?

Time Management. Is the church more focused on the next quarter or the next five years? How soon might they pull the plug on a new ministry if it's going poorly?

Mistakes. How are the mistakes and the people who make them handled? Are they chastised or accepted? Do people come together to fix a mistake, or do they step back and cast stones?

Decisions. Who makes decisions—pastor(s), other leaders, or the congregation? How important is transparency?

Risk. If you climb out on a limb, will people stand below to catch you, or wait to say, "I told you so"?

Trust. Does the congregation regard the leadership as trustworthy? Conversely, does the leadership regard the congregation as trustworthy? To what extent is micromanaging involved?

Formality. Suits and ties? Jeans and untucked shirts? How important is the appearance of the building—inside and out? How structured are the worship services?

Members. Is the focus more on events and programs or the people who populate them?[8]

There are many more. Church architecture: big steeple or strip
mall? Church branding: a hot mess or on par with Apple products?
Titles: Brother, Reverend, Doctor, or Lead Pastor?

As you become more familiar with a church, you'll likely see aspects of its personality more clearly than the people of the church can.
This is because insiders "no longer recognize these symbols on a con-
scious level."[9] Obviously, when it comes to a job search, the point is to
move beyond recognition of church personality and to assess your fit-
ness with the church and the church with you. If a preaching pastor
wears a robe to preach, you need to decide whether this attracts or
repels you. If the church has a small light show during worship, you
need to know if the church is oil and you are water.

Let me give you two examples of discovering a church's
personality from my own experience. During one interviewing weekend, the worship pastor of the church gave my young children
piggyback rides as we walked through my neighborhood. This told me
a lot about who he was and what the church valued. Another time, in
an interview with a different church, I went to lunch with the three
senior teaching pastors of their mega-church. On a Thursday at noon,
they all ordered beers—one of them ordered *two*. Some of you might
be wondering if that church is still hiring. And others, well, you're
wondering if these pastors were even Christians. This is what I mean
by personality and whether you belong.

As you interview with a church and the people you'll work most
closely with, ask whether or not you could enjoy a long road trip with
these people. This type of question becomes more critical the more
senior the position. When considering the fit of an executive pastor
and a lead pastor, church consultants Bill Easum and Bill Tenny-

---

8 This list has been adapted with light modifications from Philip Douglass, *What's Your Church's
Personality? Discovering and Developing the Ministry Style of Your Church* (Phillipsburg, NJ: P&R Publishing, 2008), 5–7.
    9 Ibid., 7.

Brittian alternatively suggest, "Would I like to spend a month isolated on a desert island with this person?"[10]

Some churches will use tools to evaluate fit. In fact, the bulk of Douglass's book is designed to do exactly this. Like the sixteen personality types of the Myers-Briggs test, Douglass crafted a test to categorize different church personalities. If you could have a church go through the evaluations, I expect it would be a helpful endeavor. My fear, however, is that the test is too involved for a candidate to ask a church to complete during the search process.

It's not uncommon for a church to ask candidates to take a personality test. They may use Myers-Briggs, DiSC, Enneagram, or something similar. These tests can be helpful but, in my opinion, they shouldn't be determinative by themselves. Results should be considered as only one part of the equation.

For example, I know of one church that found a qualified individual and moved forward with him through several stages of the process, including writing long essays, sampling his sermons, and conducting phone interviews. It was going very well—until the candidate received a link to a seven-minute personality test to assess his entrepreneurial skills. At that point, the church believed him to be fully aligned with their church-planting aptitude. Unfortunately, he didn't score high enough, and the church immediately killed the process. The test became *the* parameter instead of a helpful tool.

Ask Questions and Spend Time with the Church

The best way to discern fit and avoid a mismatch is by spending time together and asking questions. Do this over the phone, through e-mail, in person, and by whatever other means you can. "Assessment of overall match is facilitated by maximizing both the amount and the depth of your communication with the congregation."[11]

If you feel like the church isn't allowing enough time for this during the search, let them know. Perhaps they feel the pressure of the vacancy or have difficulty imagining what it might be like to be in your

---

[10] Bill Easum and Bill Tenny-Brittian, *Effective Staffing for Vital Churches: The Essential Guide to Finding and Keeping the Right People* (Grand Rapids: Baker, 2012), 127.

[11] Cionca, *Before You Move*, 100.

place. In other words, perhaps they're so focused on asking their questions that they leave little time for yours. Perhaps they have their own interests far more in view than you realize, which is a real possibility. Or perhaps they have a good feeling about you and want to expedite the process. Whatever their reasons, it won't hurt to ask them for more intentional time together. I want to stress the word *intentional*. A search process can take many months, but I'm not talking about the time accumulated by dead air during the days and weeks you're not communicating.

Spending time on the church's website and listening to lots of sermons will help. In the last two transitions I made, I listened to the previous six to nine months of sermons before I arrived. This was so helpful. Sermons have a way of reflecting who a church is and forecasting who they will be. To those considering an associate role, Jason Helopoulos offers this counsel: "You will sit under [the senior pastor's] preaching . . . If you can't [respect him] in the beginning, don't take the position."[12]

If possible, try to visit the church before you're announced as a candidate—an incognito visit, if you will. Many pastors find this a helpful way to evaluate fit. Attending a church service tends to bring more clarity than a dozen video conference calls or sermon podcasts.

Don't neglect to find ways to spend time with church members too. You want to make sure the story of the church you've heard from the staff, leaders, and search committee is the same story you hear from members. It's possible that those involved in the search are open to the changes you hope to bring. In fact, members of the search team may have joined the search committee precisely because they're dissatisfied with the *modus operandi*. In a book to help search committees find a new senior pastor, the author tells the story of one pastor who was brought in by the search committee to make changes but was surprised to learn that the "membership had no intention of seeing those changes occur."[13] Be very cautious when a search team entices you

12 Helopoulos, *The New Pastor's Handbook*, 43.
13 Frank S. Page, *Looking for a New Pastor: 10 Questions Every Church Should Ask* (Nashville: B&H, 2017), 94.

with similar words. Moving to a dysfunctional church won't sound too bad if they tell you they want you to change them. *But do they?*

A person may want to lose weight, but are they willing to do what's necessary to lose it? A pastor may want to keep up with the original languages, but is he willing to do the necessary hard work? A church may want to increase in racial and ethnic diversity, but as a candidate you need to discern if they're actually willing to share their power with those who don't look like them.

Simply put, it's healthy to have some skepticism regarding a search committee's desire to change. Attempt to learn where the real power and influence is within the church and discern if those people share the same vision for change as the search team.

I'll close by coming back to where I began this chapter. It's difficult to overstate the importance of finding the proper match when candidating with a church. Speaking to both churches and candidates, one consultant writes,

> Many church leaders, though faithful to their calling, are disillusioned with the ministries they were once certain would bring them many fruitful years of service. A significant part of this crisis stems from an incomplete and often haphazard approach to matching a church's needs with a pastoral candidate's strengths and calling. The resulting disillusionment on both sides, from unfulfilled expectations, has become an unbearable source of stress on pastors and churches in every city and town in America.[14]

Too many transplants are being rejected by the body. Therefore, when considering a job—whatever you do—don't just ask, *what does it pay?* Or *how often will I preach?* You need to ask so much more than that. No amount of pay or preaching will compensate for a transplant mismatch.

---

[14] Umidi, *Confirming the Pastoral Call*, 13.

* * *

"Temptations that Can Trick You into Taking the Wrong Job"

By William Vanderbloemen

"Good is the enemy of great." Jim Collins's words ring true in business, but also in choosing a job. People pick a job because it seems like a good choice, only to find themselves unfulfilled and wanting. Survey after survey reveals that over half of the US workforce is not happy with their job. Even vocations that are grounded in "purpose" are not immune to this trend. In a recent study we commissioned of high-growth churches and their staff, half of all pastoral staff members said they would be open to a move in the coming year. Half. And that's in fast-growing churches—nevermind the more common scenario of a stagnant or dying church.

People never set out to take jobs that leave them unhappy. They often take jobs that seem to be good ones, only to end up miserable. If you're thinking of making a career move, you should think carefully. The job you take is likely where you will spend more time than you do at home. The people you work with will see you as much as (or more than) your family.

So how do you avoid making a bad career choice? In the tens of thousands of hours I've spent helping companies hire people (and people discern their career path), I've noticed three key temptations that cause people to take the wrong job.

Because it feels good. Why wouldn't you want to top off that Ivy League degree with a job as a ski lift attendant? Sounds ridiculous, but it happens. People take jobs that they think will make them feel better. Deep inside each of us is a longing to feel fulfilled, happy, or just pleasure. And that temptation leads down some really bad paths, including choosing the wrong job. Just because a job opportunity comes up in Maui for you does not mean that God is calling you to pack up and go. By the same token, just because it may "feel" better to move away from the place you grew up, it may not be the right decision. In fact, I believe that in the end, more people end up moving near either their family or their spouse's family than not. The siren call to a feel-good opportunity may be just that, a siren call. Before taking the job, ask yourself, "Would I take this job if it didn't make me feel any better?"

Because I will make more money. I have lost count of the times I've talked to candidates who are ready to move, and take a pay cut, in order to find a job that fits their purpose. I've also lost track of how many people I've interviewed who want to leave their job but are locked into "golden handcuffs" and cannot afford to make a move. Is there value in getting a job that makes good money? Of course there is, but the point of having money is not to have more money. As my friend (and client) Dave Ramsey says, the point of having money is to have peace. So before you take a job just to get a bigger check, ask yourself, "Would I take this job if the pay were the same as what I'm making now? What if taking this job meant taking a pay cut?"

Because it will give me status. Everyone wants to climb the corporate ladder. Even the most noble companies have people seeking promotions. Seeking to be competitive and striving to do the most you can with your career are not bad goals. But far too often I talk to job seekers who have found that the power or status that came with their job either wasn't as powerful as they thought, or it came with serious baggage. Before taking a new job, be sure to ask yourself, "Would I take this job if it were a demotion from my current status?"

I have a pastor friend who says, "If there's one good thing about temptations, it's that there are no new ones." I'd venture to say that all temptations, of any kind, fall into these three buckets. But far too often folks only watch out for temptations at the moral crossroads of life. They are everywhere, including your job search.

Finding a job that makes you feel good, pays you well, and gives you status could be really awesome. But even better would be finding a job that gives you a sense of purpose and a lasting knowledge that your days are being well spent.

William Vanderbloemen is the CEO and Founder of Vanderbloemen Search Group and author of *Next: Pastoral Succession That Works*, *Search: The Pastoral Search Committee Handbook*, and *Culture Wins: The Roadmap to an Irresistible Workplace*.

ASK LOTS OF QUESTIONS

For which of you, desiring to build a tower,
does not first sit down and count the cost?
– Luke 12:28

Chapter 3 was something of a grab bag of miscellaneous job search advice. The material focused on the beginning of the process. Now that we've covered more ground, it's time to have a similar chapter for the latter stages of the hiring process.

Ask Lots and Lots of Questions

One of the most important things a candidate can do during the hiring process is ask good questions. According to one survey, over half of those who were forced out of their positions said they "didn't ask adequate questions about the church before accepting the job."[1]

Don't be afraid to ask sensitive questions that probe potential controversy and contention within a congregation. Far from avoiding these, discovering them should be your aim. It will save pain in the long run. When one pastor was interviewing with a church, he

---

[1] Anthony and Boersma, *Moving On—Moving Forward*, 141.

unknowingly hit a tender spot. At dinner with the search team in the back of a fancy restaurant, they cordially exchanged questions, and by all accounts, things were going well. Then the young pastor asked,

> If your church thought it could reach more people for Jesus by changing the name of your church—and I'm not saying at all that I want to change the name or that a name change would even help—would the church be open to this kind of change for the sake of more people hearing the gospel?

To this, the head of the search team stood up from the table. In no uncertain terms, he told the pastor he couldn't believe the nerve of the young man, that such an arrogant and impossible thing would even be suggested. Didn't he know this church had been called by its name long before some whippersnapper came around and that it would be called by its name long after? My friend thought he'd asked a simple question. *Of course you change the name.* But judging by this response, it was clear he was wrong.

Asking good questions is important not only for discovering landmines but also for showing the church you are genuinely interested and are taking the job and all it entails seriously. Asking good questions may determine whether or not you get the job, or it may determine whether the job you finally get is the one you actually want.

There's also a higher purpose to asking questions. In every conversation, even as a pastoral candidate, you're teaching people that as much as you respect God's calling on your life and as much as you are going to the new church to serve them, your ultimate and primary service is to Christ.[2]

If you need some ideas to get started, see "Appendix B: 131 Questions to Ask a Potential Employer." If you're looking for a job in a parachurch ministry, this list would also work, though with a little modifying.

---

[2] Interview with Eddie Cole, District Superintendent of the Eastern District of the Evangelical Free Church of America, May 24, 2017.

Speak to Former Employees

You should also consider speaking to former employees. You might ask questions like these:

> What were your favorite things about working at the church?
> What were some challenges?
> If you feel comfortable saying, what were the circumstances for your departure?
> Would you work there again? Why or why not?

In addition, if you know former employees are still in the area, you might want to know if they plan to still attend the church. This is particularly useful to ask of the former senior pastor. You'll want to know if the pastor who planted the church and pastored it for twenty-five years is still living down the street and showing up on Sundays. The shadow of this pastor's leadership will be strong enough as it is, and to have him still among the church could potentially be divisive—not automatically so, but potentially. "Successions from first-generation leaders to second-generation leaders are the least likely to go well. In fact, too often they end up much more like a divorce than a wedding."[3]

As you speak with a former employee, be as discerning as you can. Remember, he or she is a *former* employee, not a *current* one. If at any point the person is hesitant to answer specific questions, and you're unsure of why, you could just say something like, "If you were me, what questions should I be asking the church before I commit?" This allows the former employee to offer suggestions without having to spell out all the issues.

Send More Samples of Your Work

We recently had coffee mugs made with our church logo on them. We give them to newcomers. Before we bought 300 coffee mugs, I asked the company that made them to send me a sample. This was helpful because it allowed me to make an informed decision. Since then,

---

[3] Vanderbloemen and Bird, *Next*, 79.

however, the company keeps sending me all kinds of stuff: pens, water bottles, tote bags, and brochures—lots and lots of brochures. This has not been helpful.

Candidates should learn something from this. At the right time, and in the right amount, sending samples is helpful. But sending *too* many samples or sending them at the wrong time is not helpful.

Early in the hiring process, your cover letter package is probably enough. But as the process continues, you might want to send a few samples of things you've worked on. This doesn't mean you should send your complete series of handcrafted small group curriculum. Don't do that. Just send your favorite lesson or two.

If you're a worship leader, perhaps you'll send a sample of a devotional you led your worship team through or a few favorite worship sets with an explanation of why you enjoyed them so much. If you're in youth ministry, perhaps you have videos from events or mission trips or material from a favorite Wednesday night teaching series. If so, send those.

Again, sending high-quality samples of your work—at the right time and in the right amount—can be helpful. It'll help you stand out from the crowd.

Know When to Play the Field and When to Narrow the Search

I don't really like the dating analogy, but to a point, it fits. "Did you hear the news? Pastor John is going on a date with that church over in St. Louis. I think it's getting serious."

There's a time when it's acceptable, even expected, to be in simultaneous conversations with multiple churches. People expect this if you're a graduating seminary student, but even then you'll need to know when to cut the multiple conversations off so you can focus on just one church at a time.

There's not an exact formula, but there are some boundaries that I believe most would agree upon. If you're sending cover letters and resumes to churches, especially those doing open searches, then it's probably fine for you to be in conversation with several churches. It's like having casual conversations in the cafeteria, not holding hands over a candlelight dinner.

But you don't want to be in the place where one weekend you have the final candidating interviews at one church and the next weekend you plan to do the same at another church. There may be rare situations where both church and candidate are unsure and something like this could take place, but, generally speaking, this kind of situation helps no one. One author calls this the "horse-race strategy" and flags it as something to be avoided. He writes,

> This strategy was once a common practice. It consisted of committees inviting several preachers and allowing them to preach on a given Sunday, one after another, for several weeks. Many years ago, I had a visit from a church that I will never forget. They had identified me as one of their probable candidates and asked for me to preach as part of a month-long competition. The church would vote, and the one with the highest number of votes at the end of the month would get the job. I cannot think of a worse strategy. It ignores those very important factors beyond preaching that make a great pastor.[4]

Thankfully, this practice is now uncommon, but it's not gone away entirely. Some churches still use it. Besides over-emphasizing preaching, this leads to a divisive popularity contest with repercussions long after a pastor is called.

The further into the hiring process you are, the more your heart will become invested. Our role as candidates is to trust in the goodness and sovereignty of God and to practice the golden rule (Matt 7:12). Finding a job in Christian ministry is a spiritual endeavor that requires godliness and trust. It's not the Miss Universe competition. If you're unsure about where to draw the line between talking with many churches and talking with just one church, ask trusted friends. Don't figure this out alone. As Proverbs teaches, "In an abundance of counselors there is safety" (11:14b; cf., 15:22).

---

[4] Page, *Looking for a New Pastor*, 66.

When in doubt, err on the side of too much disclosure with a church, not too little. Rarely will this hurt your chances of future employment. And if it does, so what? You did the right thing. That's the important part, and God will be pleased.

Don't Get Desperate

All this talk of dating leads to another area of consideration: never take a job if you're fairly sure it will end poorly.

When things look bleak, there can be an understandable tendency to overlook a serious mismatch between church and candidate. Resist this. Cling to your theological convictions. God is a caring, loving Father. Remember the words of Jesus: "If you then, who are evil, know how to give good gifts to your children, how much more will your Father who is in heaven give good things to those who ask him!" (Matt 7:11). And the psalmist writes, "I have been young, and now am old, yet I have not seen the righteous forsaken or his children begging for bread" (Psalm 37:25).

If you've ever purchased a home, then you know there's nothing wrong with buying a "fixer upper." And yet, the astute home-flipper must know when to walk away. If the superficial aesthetics of a home are poor—bad carpet, dated wallpaper—that's one thing. If, however, the house's foundation is cracking, you must be willing to walk away.

When it comes to evaluating a church's health, we don't know what God might do in any given church. At the same time, God wants us to be wise. There's a difference between trusting God and testing him. Sometimes desperate people don't know the difference.

Looking for your first job can sometimes lead to desperation, which can lead to poor decisions. I know one pastor who graduated from seminary and found himself with only a few leads. Consequently, this pastor took a call to a church in need of revitalization. But he didn't ask enough questions. The foundation had cracks, and his pastorate lasted eight weeks. He and his young family had to move back in with his parents while he hesitantly opened his heart up to the possibility of another call. "In hindsight," he said, "I could have done more digging." He continues:

But I couldn't get any other [pastoral] calls. And here I am graduating from seminary. We can't afford to live in the house we are
living in, and our lease is up on our house. We had to move. I'm
watching the clock tick down; I have four more months before
we have to move; I have no call; I don't know what I'm doing with
my life. And here's this one church that's really interested.

I can commiserate. When I was graduating from seminary, I remember thinking, *A church finally wants me—me of all people!* But
when you feel this way, you'll be tempted not to ask hard, necessary
questions. They will plan a two-hour interview with only a few
minutes at the end for your questions. And you'll be fine with this because you are desperate to sell yourself to them or to anyone that will
have you. Please don't get desperate.

I know it might be difficult, but you can hold another job while
searching for a church. This is a *far* better strategy than moving to pastor a church that will leave you and your family emotionally,
spiritually, and even financially bankrupt.

If you choose to do something else besides pastoral ministry for a
season, make sure you're active in your own local church. The stamp
of approval from your local church will be necessary. There's a saying
that floats around the pastoral job search world: "Pastors with pastorates can get pastorates." In other words, if a church currently
recognizes you as a pastor, then it's at least more likely that another
church will agree with that assessment. This is not universally true;
dictums never are.

But looking for a pastoral role in ministry without currently being
a pastor sometimes raises questions: Why aren't you pastoring? Why
were you unable to find a call after seminary? And so on. These questions arise because churches are trying to discern whether or not a
candidate is qualified for ministry. So if another church has *already*
given their stamp of approval, then it takes away at least some of the
risk.

One option around this hurdle, perhaps, is to be such a faithful
member of your local church that they will happily give you an une-
quivocal recommendation.

When things aren't going well in your job search, beware of the negative effects of ego-stroking and flattery. Be patient and wait for God. Don't go work for the first church that says they'd be glad to have you. At one point in a job search, things were looking very bleak for me. After many months of looking and interviewing, I had only been able to convince one church to consider me as their pastor. *One!* I confess, the fact that I only had one option did make that option look pretty good. Beggars can't be choosers, right? Yet the more time I spent with the church, spoke with trusted friends, and prayed about it, the more I realized we would be a mess for each other. So, I told them, "Thanks, but I don't think this would be right." I had to do that without any other prospects on the horizon. You might be reading this thinking, "Wow, that took a lot of faith." At the time it seemed like a stupid thing to do. Deep down, I wondered if I was more Jonah than Joshua. Looking back, however, I know this was a spiritual victory, one that God used to stretch my faith and grow my character.

Be Gracious When You Tell Them "No"

Much of this book is about getting the right job. But as you look for the right job, at some point you'll likely have to turn a job down. When you do so, be gracious, just as you want churches to be gracious with you.

When you know it's a "no," tell them as soon as you can. Churches have other candidates they need to pursue. But before you do reject a church, remember what it's like to be rejected. Behind what might feel like their impersonal communication with you is a person made in the image of God. If in some way the church wounded you during the hiring process, your temptation will be to shame them with your words. "An eye for an eye" is not the right verse to meditate on. Consider this one instead: "Good sense makes one slow to anger, and it is his glory to overlook an offense" (Prov 19:11).

That said, if you genuinely think the search team could benefit by learning something, then you could share it. But before you hit send on that email to the search committee, I'd ask the head of the search team if they're even open to hearing a few thoughts from you. If he or she says no, move on. If they are open, then share your criticism with humility and without exaggeration.

Prepare Your Family

If you do accept a job and prepare to move, don't forget to also prepare your family. This starts during interviews. For various reasons, a church may not want to include your spouse in interviews until the end. This is a generally helpful approach because it communicates to the candidate that the church knows they aren't hiring two people for the price of one.

Jason K. Allen, president of Midwestern Baptist Theological Seminary, believes in most contexts the "buy one, get one free" model of pastor and spouse has gone away. However, he fears the pendulum sometimes swings too far the other way in that pastors have become overly protective of their spouses. He tells the story of a young pastor who "nearly torpedoed his candidacy" because he was too defensive about the role his wife would play at the church. Allen writes, "We must protect our families, but we need not sequester them."[5]

It's difficult to know the right balance. But one thing's for sure: being a pastor's wife isn't easy. Gloria Furman writes about these struggles in her book *The Pastor's Wife*. She recalls a time when an attendee urgently sought her out after the church's gathering. When she learned what was so urgent, it turned out the church's air conditioner wasn't working properly. This woman wanted her to know because—obviously—the pastor's wife needs to know.

In another place in the book she mentions how the "fishbowl feeling [of being in ministry] can take a sinister tone—like your family is the fish in the tank and everyone else is a cat." She recalls the time when, at a Christmas Eve service, a woman was disappointed that Furman wasn't bedazzled enough. "You are the pastor's wife!" she told her. "You are supposed to be the best-dressed woman here." The woman proceeded to take off her jewelry so Furman could adorn herself.[6]

I suspect most ministry wives can relate to this "fishbowl feeling." To counteract this, we need to help churches set healthy expectations

---

[5] Jason K. Allen, *Discerning Your Call to Ministry: How to Know For Sure and What to Do About It* (Chicago: Moody, 2016), 56–58.
[6] Gloria Furman, *The Pastor's Wife: Strengthened by Grace for a Life of Love* (Wheaton: Crossway, 2015), 17, 36–37, 39.

for the spouses of those in ministry. Speaking specifically to the interview process, Furman writes,

> A pastoral search committee told a friend of mine that her gifts would be "a nice bonus" to her husband's potential ministry as their pastor. Other wives are asked in pastoral interviews, "So, what ministry will you lead if your husband is hired?" Another was told that the church would consider her an effective pastor's wife if she simply permitted him to do his job and "stayed out of his way." We need God's wisdom when navigating these various ideas regarding the role of the minister's wife.[7]

Let's return to the topic of how much to involve your spouse in the interview process. When a church doesn't include the spouse early in the hiring process, it can create a situation with massive pressure on the final candidating weekend. My wife, for example, hasn't enjoyed the stress that comes from being involved in several interviews for her husband's job. But I agree with one author who writes: "It's easier for a spouse to say, 'Let's not pursue this further' after an interview than to come to that conclusion during the candidating weekend."[8] It's no light decision to consider a move, and you'll want your spouse's input, support, and encouragement from beginning to end.

When you do get to the candidating weekend, which may actually be a whole week, there will likely be several meetings and interviews set up only for you, the candidate. During these interviews, consider asking the church to set up informal events for your spouse to attend, perhaps with church members who would be peers. For example, if your spouse is a young mother, the church could set up an event with other moms in the church.

Now let's talk about when your spouse is included in the interviews. In chapter 6 I listed several questions a spouse might be asked. There are several questions I hope a church will ask a spouse. For example, "How did you become a Christian?" and "What could we do for you to help make this process as meaningful and painless as

---

[7] Furman, *The Pastor's Wife*, 74.
[8] Cionca, *Before You Move*, 131.

possible?" These are nice questions. They communicate interest, love, and support.

However, other questions are too probing for a church to ask a spouse. I listed these questions anyway because these are questions a church *might* ask, and it would be wise to be ready for them in case they do. Take this one, for example: "Do you plan to work outside the home?" A church *can* ask this, but I'm not sure it's any of their business—though that's not the answer I would suggest giving.

During one interview my wife started crying in front of forty people because of their excessively pointed questions. Needless to say, this didn't endear me to the church or the person asking the questions. In another situation my wife was asked if she was prepared to live on a pastor's salary. If asked in the right context and with the right tone, and from a loving friend or mentor, this *might* be a wonderful question. But usually it's not.

As you both interview, especially during the candidating weekend, you might encourage your spouse to jot down brief notes to discuss later. It can be difficult to remember all that's said and done during the whirlwind. These notes will prove helpful as you debrief back at the hotel each night.

Speaking of the hotel, the candidating process will be exhausting no matter what. That's why I'd encourage you to stay at a hotel rather than with a family of the church. There's a financial cost to the church, but you don't need to feel that you're unreasonably burdening them by asking. You're there to work and to evaluate a potential move, which is a weighty thing. You don't need the extra stress that comes from remaining in constant interview mode.

Of course, if you do stay with a family, you will learn a lot. But you must weigh this with needing time alone to talk honestly with your spouse and decompress. If you're going to candidate well—which the church wants you to do—you need your regular bedtime and breakfast time, especially if your candidating lasts not a weekend but a week. This is all the more necessary if you have children. Parenting in front of any audience, not to mention one sizing you up, can be exhausting. If your kids are young, pick a hotel with a pool. The distraction will be good for all of you.

This one last thing to keep in mind when preparing your family is something of a downer. If you go all the way through the hiring process to the congregational vote, be prepared for the vote to not go well. If you've made it that far, it's likely the vote will be positive.

But if it's not, remember that "no" votes—whether from individuals or, even worse, the congregation as a whole—*may* be reflections of you and your ability, but they also *may not*. These votes can be just as much a reflection of the congregation's view of the current church leadership, including the people on the search committee. If this is the case, then it's likely out of your control. In other words, it's possible that before you even arrived for the final candidating weekend, many people had already decided how they would vote. I don't mention this so that you can shirk responsibility for anything going poorly, but so that you and your family aren't crushed as you make a long and dejected return home, only to start the process over again.

With these pleasant thoughts behind us, let's turn to something not controversial at all: money.

* * *

"Know Where You're Going: Four Questions to Ask the Search Team that Go Deeper"

By Jared C. Wilson

There are questions every pastoral candidate ought to ask a search committee or hiring team when evaluating possible relocation, and then there are the questions every pastoral candidate ought to *really* ask.

By this I mean that it's fairly normal to ask about the town, the size of the church, and its basic socio-cultural demographics if such information isn't readily available. But there are questions about churches that reveal more and can better prepare pastoral candidates for effective ministry in contexts new to them. You can look up population, income per capita, ethnic demographics, etc.—and all of those things are informative—but if you really want to know where you're going, think about asking questions like these:

1. What power centers in the church should I be aware of? In other words, who's really influential in the congregation, even if it's not the other pastors or staff team members? What families are prominent? What laypeople carry a lot of weight in the church?

2. Do I have your permission to talk to the previous pastor? I would want to know what wisdom about the congregation the previous leader could share. I want to be mature and discerning enough not to take anything he says at face value, especially if he left under bad circumstances. You will want to regard every congregant on new terms and not prejudge them based on someone else's perception of conflict, but it is still worth hearing any advice about the role the previous holder can give you. And if they don't give you permission to talk to the previous pastor, ask why.

3. What significant challenges has your church faced in the last 5-10 years, and how did they overcome them? Ask them what has "marked" them in the last decade. Have they been through periods of conflict, potential or actual splits, challenging seasons of lean growth or quick growth that changed relational/cultural dynamics? What obstacles have they overcome or what successes have they accomplished that have changed the church, and what did they learn about those accomplishments?

4. What are the church's idols? Every church has a thing or set of things that dominates in rivalry for worship of God. In some churches it's family sports. In others it's religious performance or intellectualism. In others it's social standing or suburban affluence. Ask the hiring team, "What sacred cows are here? What landmines should I know about before I step on them? What unspoken rules exist in congregational life that could make people turn on me?"

Perhaps these questions have prompted new lines of inquiry of your own. The point is not to become a church's inquisitor or to pry for gossip. But if you're going to devote the next season of your ministry—or the rest of your life—to this church, it makes sense to ask deeper, probing questions that help you evaluate its identity and culture and whether you're the best man for the position.

Jared C. Wilson is the director of content strategy for Midwestern Baptist Theological Seminary and managing editor of For The

Church, Midwestern's site for gospel-centered resources. He is the author of several books, including *The Imperfect Disciple*, *The Story of Everything*, *The Prodigal Church*, and *Gospel Wakefulness*. His writing has appeared in numerous publications. His blog, *The Gospel-Driven Church*, is hosted by The Gospel Coalition, and he speaks at churches and conferences throughout the year.

TALK ABOUT MONEY

For the Scripture says, "You shall not muzzle an ox when it
treads out the grain," and, "The laborer deserves his wages."
– 1 Timothy 5:18

The Bible is replete with stories of those ensnared by the power of money. Consider the well-known Levite in Judges 17–18. To paraphrase, he is basically asked, "Young man, do you want a better preaching gig? If so, then come on up. Don't be a priest to a family; be one to a whole tribe." Previously he had worked for only a small wage, a set of clothes, and his living expenses (17:10). But when the Levite heard this new offer—albeit one made by 600 armed warriors—his "heart was glad" (Judg 18:20). Additionally, consider Balaam in Numbers 22, Gehazi in 2 Kings 5, the rich young ruler in Mark 10, Zacchaeus in Luke 19, and Ananias and his wife Sapphira in Acts 5.

We don't know the specifics of why each of these people were so captivated with money. Was it status or security? Power or pleasure? We just don't know. What we do know is that money ensnared them.

Greed can be a slippery and hidden thing. Timothy Keller writes about this in his book *Counterfeit Gods*:

Notice that in Luke 12 Jesus says, "Watch out! Be on your guard against all kinds of greed." That is a remarkable statement. Think of another traditional sin that the Bible warns against—adultery. Jesus doesn't say, "Be careful you aren't committing adultery!" He doesn't have to. When you are in bed with someone else's spouse—you know it. Halfway through you don't say, "Oh, wait a minute! I think this is adultery!" You know it is. Yet, even though it is clear that the world is filled with greed and materialism, almost no one thinks it is true of them. They are in denial.[1]

This is a good observation, but maybe the last line should read "*We* are in denial." I know I often am.

Don't Be Shy or Afraid to Talk about Money

The potential for money to become an idol makes it difficult for pastors to talk about compensation during the hiring process, especially when you add how taboo it is in our culture to discuss one's income. How many of your friends know your annual salary? Or how many of your friends' salaries do you know?

But the private nature and the potential misuse of money doesn't negate its proper use. God made money, and though we tend to abuse it (just like sex, food, and exercise), God's not uncomfortable with the material world. He made it and called it good. So don't shy away from talking about money in the final stages of a job search. Godly people can talk about money in godly ways.

After all, the church you're interviewing with has already been talking about money for many months. They likely locked in a salary range long before you even heard about the opening, which means they had to get comfortable talking about money. They shouldn't be surprised when a candidate wants to talk with them about it.

But this isn't always the case. When one pastor I know asked about money, he was scolded and told, "You never ask about money; you trust the Lord to provide." This is an over-spiritualized and even manipulative error. We don't say this to Christians in other professions. Does a doctor lack faith if she asks about her potential salary?

---

[1] Keller, *Counterfeit Gods*, 57–58.

Of course not. Another pastor I know quipped, "I do trust the Lord, but I have a hard time trusting search committees and churches. I know the Lord will provide. What I want to know is how much the Lord will provide through you . . . and whether I have to get a second job in order for him to provide."

Components of a Salary Package

Early in the hiring process, it'll probably suffice to speak in generalities. But at some point, you need to speak in more detail, even asking the church to put the entire compensation package into writing. They should be glad to do this.

In addition to base salary, here are some of the benefits and other issues related to money that you'll want to ask about:

- health insurance for the pastor and family,
- vision and dental insurance for the pastor and family,
- life and disability insurance for the pastor,
- health savings account,
- continuing education and conference money,
- money for ministry tools such as books and computer software,
- reimbursement for church-related meals,
- cell phone,
- paid holidays (how many and which days),
- sick/personal days,
- vacation (total vacation days and total Sundays off; also, do vacation days rollover to the following year?),
- retirement contribution,
- contribution to Social Security and Medicare tax contribution (FICA) and whether the assistance is given to the employee directly in paychecks or whether it's paid to the government for the employee,
- parsonage,[2]

---

[2] For several reasons the number of churches offering a parsonage (or in some traditions called a manse) has drastically decreased in the last few decades. For one, the culture of "it's okay for me

- federal minister's housing allowance,
- sabbatical policy,
- mileage or automobile reimbursement for business travel,
- performance reviews and associated yearly salary increases,
- moving and other relocation expenses,
- cost of living differences if moving from one region of the country to another,
- severance policy.

Not all of these benefits may be provided, and some that currently aren't may be offered in the future. I'd encourage you to ask about all of them, however, because you're not simply negotiating for higher pay. What you're doing in asking about compensation is seeking to arrive at clarity. Few things will cause more bitterness to you and your family (and the church) than misunderstandings about compensation.

Negotiating Your Salary Package

When it came time to discuss salary, one search committee leader told a pastor: "Here's the deal; let's just lay our cards on the table. We would like to get you here for as little as possible. You would like to come here for as much as possible. And we have to work around that." This, I suppose, is one possible way to begin the negotiation, but it neither reflects how I have ever felt about remuneration, nor how I would coach a search team to feel about money.

If you feel you need to negotiate your salary, don't hesitate only because you think asking for more money is inherently evil or unchristian. It's not. Nevertheless, it might be helpful for you to have some background on how compensation packages are determined. Some say a pastor should be paid what a local public-school teacher makes. Others say a pastor should receive the median income among their church community. Maybe, but maybe not. Good churches typically arrive at salary packages based primarily on three factors.

---

to just drop by the pastor's house" has faded. Also, the economic advantages of a parsonage to the pastor are nearsighted; equity in a home is often a person's largest financial investment in the future. In addition, "the family has no guarantee of housing if the pastor dies or becomes disabled" (*Pastor Search Committee Handbook, Revised,* 50). That's not an appealing prospect.

First, salary is influenced by ***the job itself***. A good church will consider things like the job description and its associated responsibilities, the size of the church and surrounding community, and other economic factors particular to the area.

Second, salary is influenced by ***the employee's competency***. A good church will consider whether the person is overqualified or underqualified for the job. They'll consider whether the person has fifteen months or fifteen years of experience and whether the person has a Bible college degree or a doctorate.

Finally, salary is influenced by ***the financial needs of the employee***. Is the employee single or married? If he or she has children, how many? What if one of them has special needs? Alternatively, what if the employee was previously a lawyer or a doctor or a successful salesman? A wise candidate in this position will already know he or she might experience a pay cut, but a good church will seek to make the disparity less drastic.

As I mention this final category of need, perhaps you're worried that because you're young and single a church will try to hire you for cheap. They could. In fact, some churches *will*. Moreover, I'm sure some churches never adjust salary based on metrics. They just keep paying the new guy what they paid the last guy, regardless of any other factors. But healthy churches typically set the salary based on the first two categories (role and competency), and then only adjust upward (not downward) as necessary to meet personal needs.

In addition to these considerations, a candidate should also keep in mind that one's salary is *not* the total expense the church incurs in order to bring him or her on staff. Depending on benefits, these costs are perhaps 50 percent or more of an employee's taxable income. For example, a pastor's salary of $50k (including housing) likely costs the church around $75k by the time they include primary benefits. When you add medical insurance (which for a young family might be $1,500 per month); small insurance policies for life, dental, and disability; a Health Savings Account; employer-paid taxes such as Social Security and Medicare; and retirement benefits, say, a 5 percent match—it all adds up. This doesn't even include things like conference money, books, a computer, office space, travel reimbursement, and other miscellaneous expenses. This is why in "most churches the largest share of the annual budget goes to staff salaries."[3]

With all this in mind, let's come back to salary negotiation. If you do need to negotiate, you should do so because you feel the salary you were offered is out of step with one or more of the categories mentioned above. Has your research indicated that associate pastors of a medium-sized church in an affluent community warrant a larger salary? If so, then humbly ask. Do you think you're highly qualified for the role? If so, then humbly ask for a salary listed in the upper portion of the salary range. Are their life circumstances and needs that would make the salary they offered unworkable? Did the church simply not keep up with regular raises for the previous pastor and therefore the salary is no longer tenable?

These are rational requests, and conversation about them should also be relatively easy. It's only when you bring an ego or ignorant expectations to the table that negotiations become ugly. John Cionca notes, "A fair wage is not one that supports all of our financial wants and perceived needs. . . . I know pastors who have requested salary adjustments because they purchased a new car . . . or enrolled a child in a Christian school."[4] These requests, while in a sense are related to need, are unrealistic. If those who worked in the business world had made "similar requests (e.g., asking for a $4,000 salary increase to pay tuition at a Christian school), they would have been ridiculed."[5]

Other Things to Consider While Negotiating

Also, make sure you have a conversation about start date. This is important for several reasons. The new church likely has expectations about this, and you need to know them. It's possible to get excited about a church too soon, and your heart begins to imagine what it would be like to pastor there well before the church has given you an indication this could happen.

As an interview process continues, it's important to think through the details of leaving your current situation. You'll want to consider

---

[3] Easum and Tenny-Brittian, *Effective Staffing for Vital Churches*, 13.
[4] Cionca, *Before You Move*, 55–56.
[5] Ibid.

how long your current church might want you to stay around. If you're a youth pastor, they might want you to finish the school year. You might have the same desire if you have your own children in school.

Also consider your living situation. A move within the same city is less challenging than moving across the country. If you're renting your home, gather information about when your lease expires and how much money it takes to get out of your contract early. This will likely mean losing your security deposit, which is typically the cost of one or two months' rent. If you own a home, consider how long it might take to sell it and what you'll do if it doesn't sell right away.

These and other factors influence your potential start date. Ideally, you'll have a healthy relationship with your current employer, and they'll work with you to create a mutually beneficial timeline.

But let's face it: you're leaving, and there are reasons for it. So as you talk with the new church, discuss what might happen should your current employer decide to terminate you immediately upon announcing your intention to leave. In that situation you'll want to know whether or not you can begin working immediately for the new church. Moving is expensive, and you don't want to get caught in a situation without income.

It's also wise to have a conversation with your current employer about any other negotiated compensation that could be ambiguous as you leave, such as vacation or insurance coverage. You don't want to leave without medical coverage, especially if there will be a delay between the two employers. As I said above, don't rely on verbal conversations. Get everything in writing—not so you'll have ammunition for a lawsuit if things go south, but so everyone can arrive at clarity on the front end rather than sorting it out after the fact.

Resources on Compensation

If you need resources to help you determine a reasonable compensation package, there are several places to turn. First off, if you know any senior or executive pastors, talk to them. They can give you good advice on what they might pay someone with experience and education similar to your own. Also, you can search online for "pastor pay" (or "youth pastor pay" or "worship pastor pay," etc.) and get lots of leads. As a rule of thumb, though, remember to vet the information for reliability.

Finally, you can turn to books for help. A book full of simple but sturdy advice is *The Minister's Salary* by Art Rainer.[6] In it, Rainer discusses common pitfalls ministers make concerning money, such as neglecting retirement planning, not understanding minister's housing allowance, and what it means to opt out of Social Security.[7] In the final chapter he writes, "Do not walk this journey alone. Too much is at risk . . . Find a trusted advisor to work with on your personal finances."[8] Rainer's book is full of wise and biblical principles.

If you need a resource focused more on numbers and data (lots and lots of data), you might try the *Compensation Handbook for Church Staff* by Richard R. Hammar. It's been the definitive book on the topic for years. The newest edition is only sold on his website,[9] though previous editions can be found elsewhere. If you're interested in the specifics of current tax law for ministers, check out *Worth's Income Tax Guide for Minsters* by Beverly J. Worth.

Whatever you do, don't ignore discussing money simply because it's awkward. During pre-marital counseling, when my wife and I discuss delicate subjects with couples, I repeatedly say, "It's only awkward if we make it that way." The same will be true for you as you talk about money with a prospective church.

---

[6] Art Rainer, *The Minister's Salary: And Other Challenges in Ministry Finance* (Nashville: Rainer, 2015).

[7] To contribute to Social Security or to opt out is no small decision. It catches many new pastors off guard because they were not prepared to make the decision, nor were they even aware that a decision must be made. I'm not going to provide advice here, but make sure you know what you are doing and why you are doing it. For all effective purposes, the decision is permanent.

[8] Rainer, *The Minister's Salary*, 112.

[9] store.churchlawtodaystore.com/20cohaforchs.html.

* * *

"What's the Best Way for Pastors to Negotiate Salary?"

By Dave Harvey

A pastor talking salary can be awkward stuff. Annual incomes are, after all, the things of earth; unspiritual and unbecoming—far from the meditations of the heavenly minded minister. Or so it seems. Why not just parade his sex life before the elders too!

In the world of wages, pastors inhabit some pretty conflicted space. On the one hand, a pastor must "manage his household well" (1 Tim 3:4). This certainly includes managing finances in such a way that bills are paid and the family is clothed, fed, and able to travel in a dependable car made in the twenty-first century. On the other hand, a pastor must not be "a lover of money" (1 Tim 3:3). We can expect "enough" (1 Cor 9:8–11), yet we can't be greedy for gain (Titus 1:7)—a distinction far easier to espouse than discern. The church should desire an unmuzzled pastor (1 Tim 5:18), yet the pastor can't determine what muzzled means.

It's the "salary strain," an occupational hazard that seems to come with ministry. If navigated unwisely, it can introduce suspicion and stall the church's momentum toward the future.

So what's the best way for a pastor to negotiate his salary? Here are a few thoughts I hope will be helpful. Salary negotiations move toward wisdom when the pastor . . .

Knows his heart is always engaged in matters of money (Matt 6:21). One's salary is not a unique, amoral, heart-free zone where our desires or fears become suddenly irrelevant. The pastor should speak to God first and often when negotiating his salary. This will help him approach the process as a disciple desiring to receive God's provision and not a professional seeking to grab what he can.

Knows the church is neither suffering nor being excessively frugal in the offer extended to him. As a shepherd in God's church, we are never ambivalent over how the church's spending affects the church's stability. Yet we also don't want to feel like the church is saving money at a cost to our family. If your salary triggers concern on either side of this tension, consider it an invitation from the Holy Spirit for further discussion. In some cases, it may even be a reason to decline a role.

Knows his income may grow if the church grows and may shrink if the church experiences hard times. These realities are neither carnal nor unfair but are simply a slice of real life in the local church. In my thirty-plus years of ministry, I've been in times of both growth and decline. I've taken salary raises; I've declined raises, I've endured deductions, and I've disputed benefits. Through all these seasons I've discovered the local church is a dynamic, resilient, vulnerable, organized organism. Salary offers should be accompanied by seatbelts. By accepting the role, you agree to buckle up and adapt to the unpredictable adventures ahead.

Knows the offer accompanies the faith and enthusiasm of those extending it. This is just obvious street-smarts. If the church's leadership team or search committee is not excited about you in the role, or your arrival is going to divide the church, perhaps it's wiser to keep looking. Yes, God may call some men to churches where their doctrine or vision may polarize the people. But you'd better be certain there is a committed core of gospel-loving, doctrinally driven, courageous folk who are going to support you through the coming storm. Absent that, you're merely postponing your job search in another twelve to eighteen months and eliminating a solid reference from your last place of employment.

Knows he should communicate gratitude for the offer, even if he is unable to accept it. Someone, perhaps many, undoubtedly spent time collaborating and working to pull together this offer. A wise candidate will appreciate the effort even if he cannot accept the position or salary.

As you seek to navigate these tensions, do so remembering this remarkable reality: The final reward for your role is not delivered in your monthly paycheck. Ultimately, you serve the church with another Day in view. "And when the chief Shepherd appears, you will receive the unfading crown of glory" (1 Pet 5:4). Pastor or pastoral candidate, as you negotiate your salary, remember the unfading crown of glory. Let it inspire your humility and restrain your entitlement. Let it fill every salary discussion (or dispute!) with the knowledge that there is no sacrifice for God made in the present that will not be richly compensated by God in the future.

Dave Harvey serves as the executive director of Sojourn Network and as teaching pastor at Summit Church in Naples, Florida. He is the author of *When Sinners Say I Do*, *Am I Called*, *Rescuing Ambition*, and *Letting Go*. He is also the founder of *AmICalled.com*, a leadership resource site helping pastors, leaders, and men who sense a call to ministry.

PART THREE

FINISHING *The* RACE

DON'T *Just* SEND A RESUME

FINISH STRONG

I have fought the good fight,
I have finished the race,
I have kept the faith.
– 2 Timothy 4:7

I love watching professional cycling.

The scandals revolving around performance-enhancing drugs, however, haven't helped the sport's reputation. And even for those who are willing to forgive and forget, many still see cycling as hours and hours of seemingly uneventful action.

I understand these sentiments, but I disagree. I love the so-called boring parts, and I love the dramatic finishes. Exhibit A: Stage 16 of the 2016 Tour de France. After 130 miles and almost four and a half hours, the difference between first and second place came down to the width of a wheel spoke.

Peter Sagan won the race. He's one of the best cyclists in the world, especially at sprinting, so his win wasn't necessarily a surprise. But how he won this race can be instructive to us.

When racers began to sprint for the finish line, Sagan was right there with the leaders. As the sprint unfolded, it didn't appear like he was going to win. Another rider named Alexander Kristoff was out in front. In fact, Kristoff was doing so well that not only did spectators think he was going to win but after he crossed the line, Kristoff actually thought he won. *Cycling News* put it this way:

> The brief moment of jubilation that Kristoff experienced, thinking he had won the stage, quickly turned to more disappointment as the review of the cameras showed Sagan pushing in front of Kristoff by millimeters.[1]

What happened? How did Sagan win?

At the last second, Peter Sagan won the race because he lunged his bike over the finish line. This technique is common in cycling. Sprinters practice it all the time. But for one reason or another, Kristoff didn't lunge, either because he misjudged the distance to the finish line or assumed he had the stage in the bag. Regardless of the reason, he stopped riding hard a moment too soon.

This type of narrow victory often happens in sports. Think of how many swimming races come down to the final few strokes. Michael Phelps won his 2008 gold medal in the 100m by a mere one hundredth of a second (50.58 to 50.59).

The point for our purposes is this: yes, you have to smoke the curve, but you also have to finish all the way to the end. The difference between getting the right job and almost getting the right job might come down to the final lunge. If your job search has been progressing according to the topics covered in this book, then you're almost done. The finish line is in sight.

But you're not done yet. Before you leave your current role, you need to finish like a champion and then also start like a champion in your new role.

Before You Leave, Finish like a Champ

When I was thirteen, I ran a local 5k. At the start of the race, some kid ran full-speed for the first 100 yards. I passed him at 150 yards and so

---

[1] "Tour de France: Sagan wins in Berne: Kristoff celebrates too early, Froome stays in yellow," *CyclingNews*, July 24, 2018, http://www.cyclingnews.com/races/tour-de-france-2016/stage-16/results/.

did everyone else. The next day, however, he got his picture on the front page of the paper. I remember being really mad about it.

Marriages can start well, pastorates can start well, and so can the Christian life. Consider Solomon in the Old Testament (1 Kgs 3; 11:1–8) or Demas in the New Testament (Col 4:14; Phm 1:4; 2 Tim 4:10). They seem to have started well only to fail at what really counts: finishing well.

At this point in the job process, having put all the previous coaching into practice, you're likely in the process of a transition. Maybe you even have your house on the market and are looking at new homes in another city. This is exciting.

Yet planning for and making this transition is hard work, and in the midst of it you may find it easy to neglect your current role. You may neglect to finish well.

I remember how busy I was when I found my first job in a local church. After I accepted the offer, I still had to finish my final exams, complete projects at work, and make updates on my home. This was hard work. There was a lot to do. But difficultly is irrelevant. God calls us to finish like a champion. As Cionca notes, "A hireling hits the road focused only on the next job and paycheck, but a shepherd departs with a show of concern for the flock's well-being."[2]

I've worked in several places, and it's always telling to see if someone finishes well. Those are the memories that seem to last. Did he simply coast to the finish line, collecting paychecks but not actually working? Or did he finish all his responsibilities and tie up loose ends, taking the time to make sure no one would be left with unfinished projects? I agree with William Vanderbloemen and Warren Bird when they write: "People will remember how you leave long after they forget what you did while you were there."[3]

To paraphrase Paul, if possible, so far as it depends on you, leave in such a way that the church would call you back to work for them in the future.

Finishing well might mean you request an exit interview with church leaders. Transitions can be times of great learning, even if it's

---

[2] Cionca, *Before You Move*, 206.
[3] Vanderbloemen and Bird, *Next*, 140.

sometimes painful. By skipping the exit interview, valuable information could be lost to both you and the church. Joseph Umidi suggests church leadership should ask these questions upon an employee's departure:

1. How was our church family different from what you expected when you first came?
2. How are we as leaders different from what you expected?
3. What do you perceive to be our main strengths?
4. What changes do you believe our church body should make?
5. Were there any goals you had hoped to accomplish but didn't?
6. What would have helped you accomplish those goals?
7. What agenda do you think we should complete before we call a new pastor?
8. How do you perceive your relationship with this church family after you leave?
9. Is there anything else you would like to share with us?[4]

Keep in mind, though, if *you* are the one who suggested the exit interview, the buy-in from your church leadership might be low. It will be more edifying if you remember that an exit interview "is not a time for recrimination, argument, or hashing out issues. After all, [you've] already decided to leave."[5] Therefore, make sure your departing conversations don't become self-serving gripe sessions. Instead, focus less on problems and more on solutions that might protect others from trouble in the future.

In summary, it says a lot about us and our God when we finish strong. But regardless of who our employer is, we must never forget that we ultimately work for the Lord, and therefore we should work heartily unto him (Col 3:23). Too often, pastors don't finish strong. But the Lord expects more from us.

---

[4] Umidi, *Confirming the Pastoral Call*, 19–20.
[5] Ibid, 20.

* * *

"7 Common Mistakes Search Committees Make"[6]

By Kevin DeYoung

It seems like at any given time I'm either *on* a search committee, giving advice to those *leading* a search committee, or talking with friends going through a process *with* a search committee. Every church has had a search committee before, and almost every pastor has worked with search committees in the past. Search committees are a part of how most of us do church. Sometimes they're great, sometimes not so much.

In my experience, search committees are usually made up of hard-working, godly laypeople trying to do the best they can to serve their church. But even mature, sincere Christians can make mistakes when they are working on a task they've never done before. Here are seven common mistakes search committees make (and I'm thinking here especially of pastoral search committees):

1. Overcompensating for the previous pastor's weaknesses. This is the classic search committee blunder. Pastor Smith was a great preacher, but kind of prickly, so basically what we are looking for in our next pastor is Ronald McDonald. Don't do the pendulum swing. Every pastor has strengths and weaknesses. It's fine to want to address some problem areas from the last "administration." But don't forget what the last guy did really well. If you want to do the search process often, then let a bad experience or a bad character trait determine your next hire.

2. Mishandling internal candidates. What do you do when a current staff member is interested in your church's pastoral vacancy? That's tricky. There is no right answer for every situation, but the right process can help.

When churches have a man on their staff who is well respected, well loved, has been effective in ministry, and has the gifts for the

---

[6] This article originally appeared on *The Gospel Coalition* website and is used with permission. Although primarily addressed to search teams, it contains valuable insights for candidates. "7 Common Mistakes Search Committees Make," July 7, 2016, https://www.thegospelcoalition.org/blogs/kevin-deyoung/7-common-mistakes-search-committees-make/.

job, there is no need to go through a long search process just to show you've done your homework. Hopefully you did your homework when you brought the guy on in the first place.

This doesn't mean every internal candidate is the best man for the job. Often they don't have the gifts or calling to move from their current responsibilities to a new position. But in most cases, I think churches know that without a lengthy search. Don't string anyone along, either the internal guy you aren't going to pick, or the outside guys you are talking to, just to give the search committee legitimacy.

The bottom line: Be candid. Don't over promise. Be clear with the candidate and the congregation about how things are going to work.

3. Communicating too little. I've said before that a search committee should not be a stealth committee. Communicate early and often, with the congregation and with all prospective candidates. Even if you can't give specifics, you can tell the congregation, "We are still putting the job description together," or "We are gathering names to consider," or "We have narrowed the field down to three candidates."

Likewise, those who have expressed an interest in the position do not expect insider information, just basic courtesy. Acknowledge that you've received their forms. Let them know when they can expect to hear from you again. Give them a sense of your timetable. They are thinking through a major life change. Keep them in the loop.

4. Taking lots of time just because. No doubt, some search committees rush through the process, imagining everything will fall apart without a pastor (it won't; we're not that important). But I think the opposite danger is more common: taking a lot of time for no reason in particular. Some search committees meet too infrequently to ever gain much momentum. Others insist on listening to sermons from all 200 candidates. Narrowing down the field is hard work. It may mean difficult phone calls or disagreement on the committee. It's always easier to keep pondering your choices for another month. And sometimes committees feel like their work won't seem legitimate unless it takes a really long time. How long should the search process be? As long as it takes for you to find the right man for the job. Don't make it shorter or longer than that.

5. Crafting an impossible job description. Many churches are looking for the same pastor: an amazing preacher and visionary leader who is great with people, a gifted administrator, a fruitful evangelist, a missions champion, good with kids, beloved by the elderly—a young dynamic pastor who somehow also has 20 years experience. Get real.

Here's a better approach: make high character and shared convictions non-negotiable, then prioritize preaching, then make sure he has basic people skills, after that figure out the two or three other things that are really important in your context. It's great to set the bar high, just so long as real, non-divine people can clear it.

6. Failing to check references. It's baffling how search committees can be so thorough when it comes to theological questions, sermon listening, and umpteen phone interviews, but then fail to check with the people that know the candidate best. You should always talk to the man's wife, not to grill her as if she were applying for a job too, but to learn about their marriage and how she feels about ministry.

Likewise, you should always talk to someone who has worked with, for, or above the man you are seeking to hire. People aren't going to change dramatically from one job to the next, especially the older they get. What they were in one church is what they will be in the next church. It happens too often: churches find out six months later that their new pastor can't administrate his way out of a paper bag, or he can't get along with his colleagues, or he plays 72 holes of golf every week, or his marriage is a mess. Of course, you can't remove all risks, but a couple commonsense phone calls can save your church a world of hurt.

7. Expecting all the best candidates to come to you. In most cases, the search committee will post the job opening on the relevant denominational, educational, and third-party sites. Then they will wait and see how many applicants come in. For some positions, that may mean sifting through five applications. For the senior pastor position of an established church, that may mean hundreds of names. And you could very well have the name you need among those applicants.

But don't be afraid to knock on doors. It's not about poaching pastors or stroking egos. It's just common sense. Some of the best pastors are probably happily and effectively serving their church at the moment. They aren't looking around. But as a search committee you are. It doesn't hurt to ask (provided you do it humbly and with the utmost attention to confidentiality). No one knows what you are looking for better than you do, so get looking.

Kevin DeYoung is the senior pastor at Christ Covenant Church in Matthews, North Carolina. He is an assistant professor at Reformed Theological Seminary and the author of several books, including *Just Do Something*, *Crazy Busy*, and *The Biggest Story*.

RESTART STRONG

I ... urge you to walk in a manner worthy of the calling ...
eager to maintain the unity of the Spirit.
– Ephesians 4:1, 3

Fire someone, maybe two people. Make sure one of them is a single mother. Change the name of the church. Sell the pipe organ. Buy electric drums and a fog machine. Switch the times of the church services. Move facilities. Take all your vacation.

You can file all of these in a single category called "things not to do when you begin a new pastorate." Okay, maybe the lease at your rented facility is up, and you do have to move. Still, try not to burn the hymnals and fire the single mother.

In Your First 100 Days, Start Strong All Over Again

Scott Daniels, in his guide to help pastors as they start over in new churches, speaks of the importance of the first hundred days in a new role. Daniels compares this to the first hundred days of a presidency, noting that this has been the standard measurement of presidential flurry since Franklin D. Roosevelt took office in 1933.

In the midst of the Great Depression, FDR entered the Oval Office with a great deal of political capital as Americans were anxious for change.... During those first three months the president paved the way for major changes in banking, agriculture, industry, and public works. It only took FDR a hundred days to put the framework of the New Deal into place. Fairly or unfairly, the initial impact of all American presidents after him has been judged by the standard set by Roosevelt and his administration.[1]

Roosevelt must have drunk Red Bull for breakfast.

Daniels goes on, however, to point out a significant difference between pastors and presidents: presidents have political capital to spend. An elected president usually comes "into office with a great deal of momentum [and] authority." Pastors, on the other hand, don't. Sure, they likely begin with "a fair amount of goodwill from the congregation but... the ability to influence significant social and structural change ... largely has to be earned."[2] Zack Eswine says, "Trust takes time and faithfulness. It cannot be demanded by accepting a call or cajoled by credentials."[3]

My father, who has often served as a lay-elder in local churches, has made several transitions during his business career. During my most recent pastoral transition, he challenged me to think about what I wanted to accomplish during my first hundred days. I'm so glad he did. I had to look up the specifics to remember the details, but during my first hundred days (from Thursday, March 6 to Friday, June 13, 2014), I focused on three things: high-quality public ministry, listening and serving, and instituting a pattern of sustainable ministry.

For many reasons, the last item was most important to me. Though I wasn't even sure what sustainable ministry would look like, I knew I didn't want my pastoral ministry to be like a sparkler—bright yet brief. I wanted to be a lighthouse, one who stands against the waves over the long haul. During those first few months at my new

---

[1] T. Scott Daniels, *The First 100 Days: A Pastor's Guide* (Kansas City, MO: Beacon Hill Press, 2011), 14.

[2] Ibid., 15.

[3] Zack Eswine, *The Imperfect Pastor: Discovering Joy in Our Limitations through a Daily Apprenticeship with Jesus* (Wheaton: Crossway, 2015), 220.

church, I needed to establish a rhythm that worked over the long haul—for myself, my family, and my church.

When you begin your next role, your focus will likely have a different emphasis than mine. That's appropriate. My concern isn't that you copy me or any other pastor (and certainly not FDR). My concern is that you have a plan that's been thoughtfully and prayerfully crafted with the help of a few other people and then, once it's been set, that you stick to the plan.

To get you thinking in the right direction, here are nine ideas to consider as you start your new pastorate.

1. Strive for Unity

Pursuing unity isn't just a shrewd pastoral move; it's biblical.

Ordinarily, however, we don't simply drift toward unity. As Paul writes, we must be eager for it:

> I therefore, a prisoner for the Lord, urge you to walk in a manner worthy of the calling to which you have been called, with all humility and gentleness, with patience, bearing with one another in love, *eager* to maintain the unity of the Spirit in the bond of peace. (Eph 4:1–3)

When we're not eager for unity, our sin pulls us in the opposite direction, toward "discord, jealousy, fits of rage, selfish ambition, slander, gossip, arrogance and disorder" (2 Cor 12:20b). It would have been a tough calling to spend your first hundred days in the ancient city of Corinth. But all churches, like all Christians, have some Corinth in them—sometimes a little, sometimes a lot.

Moreover, unity isn't just biblical in an abstract sense. It's the Trinitarian *telos* of gospel ministry. As shepherds and teachers, we equip the saints in a local church for the work of the ministry, to build up "the body of Christ until we all attain to the *unity* of the faith and of the knowledge of the Son of God" (Eph 4:12–13).

But please remember that uniformity isn't (necessarily) unity. As a pastor, you can toss your weight around to get carpet the color you like or the worship music you prefer. If you're a dynamic leader and the church is desperate, you might even get more than this. But dragging people toward consensus is not the same thing as building unity, and it will never work for the long haul. It's difficult for a congregation to sing "your" songs with their jaws clenched.

Again, unity is more than people in the same place, doing the same thing. Unity occurs when we prize the glory of God above our own agendas and when we have the humility and self-awareness to know that our agenda and God's glory aren't the same thing. Striving for unity that brings glory to God means looking not only to our own interests but especially to the interests of those who were at the church before we got there and might be there after we're gone (Phil 2:4).

Here's an example of what I'm talking about, though perhaps a little pedestrian. At our church we have a small café where people gather before, between, and after services. In this café we serve a particular brand of coffee, a brand that will remain nameless. We have a whole storage shelf stacked with shiny bags of this coffee. We do this because many of our people love this brand. I, however, don't. And neither do several of my co-workers. So, I'm sure it wouldn't take too much campaigning to change the coffee brand to the one we prefer. In fact, we might even be able to just stop buying that kind and buy mine instead. As they say, I know a guy.

But why? Who cares—*really*? If I want a different coffee, I'll make it at home or buy it before church. This is what you'd tell a churchgoer, wouldn't you, if he or she complained about the church's coffee selection? So why do we pastors sometimes feel the need to have it our way on the small stuff? When we do, it dilutes our ability to shepherd the church on the big stuff.

Here are a few more suggestions on creating unity:

Don't change staff or service times. If either must be done, do it only for the sake of unity. And if you add a weekly staff meeting or you incorporate a time of prayer into an existing meeting, do so for unity, not merely because it's what you did at your last church.

Consider teaching on the church's *current* mission-vision statement, not the one you think they need, or again, the one you're bringing from your last church. I heard about one pastor who came to his new church where the interim pastor had been teaching through the Gospel of Mark. This new pastor chose to write his candidating sermon to fit the series, and after he was hired, proceeded to continue the series until the book was finished. This kind of eagerness for unity sent a clear message: The new pastor didn't believe that God began to work with this church only after he arrived.

If the church logo and church website are atrocious (and many are), let it rest a while. And when you do update your branding, consider commissioning gifted people within the church, either by allowing them to create it or to oversee the company that does.

You get the point. Unity matters to God, and in Christ it's already something we have, which is why we are exhorted to maintain it. This leads into the rest of the tips on your first hundred days. All of which are really just ways to help you strive for unity in your new church.[4]

2. Become a Good Listener

Lots of listening will make more of an impact than lots of speaking.

In this regard, I encourage you to do what one executive pastor did when he arrived at a new church. The first thing he did was set up an individual meeting with every staff member, elder, and key volunteer. At a big church—one large enough to have an executive pastor—that's a lot of meetings, but it was worth it. He spent this time asking each person the following questions:

1. Pretend I am a new attendee on a Sunday and you have just a few minutes to tell me about your ministry. What would you tell me?
2. In terms of when you work and on what days, what is your weekly schedule?
3. How is your week filled, or what does your typical week look like? What are your primary roles and responsibilities?
4. What are you passionate about in your role?
5. What was your favorite task/role/project in the past twelve months and why? What made it so special? What made it successful?

---

[4] I just used the phrase, "your church." But we have to be so careful with possessive pronouns when referring to church, don't we? "I will build *my* church," says the one who died for it.

6. What was your least favorite task/role/project in the past twelve months and why? What made it so?
7. What would make your life easier here (systems, processes, equipment)?
8. What do you want to accomplish in your ministry over the next three months? Next year?
9. How do you like to be managed? Are there any management styles or personalities that you don't do well with?
10. How do you like to be recognized and supported for your efforts?
11. What do you need from me?
12. Do you have any questions for me?

Again, this was time consuming, but it provided valuable information and began friendships.

Similarly, chat with people out of the office. Go to lunch or coffee. Grab two or three people at a time. This will help your time together feel less like a formal examination.

Once you move and settle in, it might be wise to host a meal for the search team. With all the interviews behind you, the pressure to perform should be gone. A meal together can celebrate everyone's hard work and the kindness of God that was manifested throughout the process.

One final word of caution. Don't listen to everything people tell you as the new pastor. People "who seem to enjoy being critical of the previous three pastors will more than likely get great joy out of being critical about you in the not-so-distant future."[5] As a wise man once said, "Do not pay attention to every word people say, or you may hear your servant cursing you—for you know in your heart that many times you yourself have cursed others" (Eccl 7:21–22).

In summary, be a good listener, which requires a closed mouth and a discerning mind.

---

[5] Daniels, *The First 100 Days*, 43.

3. Know and Honor Your Church's History

It's rightly been said that congregations "are not blank slates simply waiting for a new pastor to write a totally new story.... The congregation is a living, breathing cauldron of ministry and story and mission and tragedy."[6]

A new pastor must listen not only to the present but also the past. Knowing the history of your church will help you make an effective transition. If this doesn't happen—when leaders bobble the torch-pass—sometimes people get burned, and sometimes the fire goes out. This was the hard lesson learned by a young king named Rehoboam.

As you learn the history of your new church, you'll want to focus on things such as the congregation's origin; its important leaders and heroes; the glory days and what made them such; missionaries the church supports (especially if they grew up in the church); significant crises and how they were resolved; significant hopes and dreams that have been reached; building projects left incomplete; and the key families and individuals (both those who have left and those who are still around).[7]

Perhaps the place to start, though, is by finding ways to honor the most recent pastor and the work God did through him. In *Next: Pastoral Succession that Works*, the authors list several ways to do this, such as providing public opportunities for the outgoing pastor and board members to say goodbye; giving people within the church outlets to express their feelings (joy and thankfulness as well as sadness and grief); creating events to celebrate the outgoing pastor's faithful ministry; and most especially, devoting resources to honor the pastor's spouse, an oft-neglected but important move.[8]

Learning your church's history will also help you discover areas that are resistant to change. "These may include the structure of the service, the choir, the bell on the top of the church and the prayer in the middle of the week, or the color of the paint in the sanctuary."[9] I know one church that had serious objections to moving the lectern

---

6 Mead, *A Change of Pastors*, 46.
7 Adapted with a few additions from Umidi, *Confirming the Pastoral Call*, 91–92.
8 Vanderbloemen and Bird, *Next*, 173.
9 Helopoulos, *The New Pastor's Handbook*, 74.

they used for announcements. In another church, moving the American flag off the stage was a huge deal. (So the pastor moved it an inch or two each week until no one noticed it was gone . . . that is, until Memorial Day.)

Take the time to learn your church's story. It will show them you care and might even help you avoid stepping on landmines.

4. Do the Things You (and They) Do Well

In your new role, rather than changing things, it will be more important to just do what both of you—pastor and church—know how to do well and do that for a while. If it ain't broke, leave it alone.

If this means you repurpose an old sermon series from a previous church so you can focus on all the other things you need to do during the first hundred days, go for it. You won't keep this up for years, but if it helps you at first there's nothing wrong with it. If you're the worship pastor and you desire for the pool of songs to be expanded, great. But broaden the song selection slowly. At first only play the songs your musicians and congregation are comfortable with until they're comfortable with you.

5. Establish Healthy Patterns and Boundaries

There's a phrase in endurance sports called "burning matches." For every racer, there's an average pace that gets her to the finish line the fastest. And every time she increases her speed above this average pace, perhaps to catch one competitor or drop another, she "burns a match." This is part of racing, but the smart racer knows she has a finite number of matches to burn before her box is empty.

The same is true with pastoring. When you need to, you can sprint. The first hundred days might be a good time to lift your pace, but you can't sprint the whole marathon. Slow and steady—with a few strategic bursts—is far more likely to win this often-grueling endurance race.

It's not as though we don't have boundaries and limitations anyway. There are only twenty-four hours in a day and only seven days in a week. Furthermore, you can only be in one place at a time. We can't go more than three days without water or a few dozen days without food.

God has given us boundaries and limitations. The *omni*-attributes (omnipresence, omnipotence, etc.) belong to God and God alone. Ministry isn't about one superhuman helping others become superhuman, but one human helping other humans to recover their true humanity by delighting and depending on Jesus.[10] It's Satan who claims to offer a ministry without limitations: "You will be like God," he promises. "Just fall down and worship me, and you'll be so productive and famous you'll have all the kingdoms of the world and their glory."

But we won't be like God, at least not in these ways. As long as we exist, so will our limitations. Therefore, nightly sleep and weekly Sabbaths are declarations of faith that God is God and we are not. We are *his* creatures, and being his creatures is very good (Gen 1:31). Zack Eswine writes,

> You were never meant to repent because you can't fix everything. You were meant to repent because you've tried. Even if we could be god for people and fix it all, the fact remains that Jesus does not have the kind of fixing in mind that you and I want. . . . Sickness, death, poverty, and the sin that bores into and infests the human being will not be removed on the basis of any human effort, no matter how strong, godly, or wise that effort is.[11]

Therefore, pick a time to leave the office each day and stick to it. Years ago I got in the pattern of coming home around 4:30 pm, and that's still what I do; it's when my family expects me. Also, establish your non-working days and stick to it, excluding the occasional wedding or funeral. Many pastors choose either Monday or Friday as their day off, along with Saturday.

Additionally, set the number of nights a week you'll (typically) go back out for work. If your number is three or four, you can have a week where you're out six nights, but you can't do this week after week. If you need to keep track of the hours you've worked so they don't get out of hand, then do that. On the nights you are home, put your phone

---

[10] Definition of ministry adapted from Eswine, *The Imperfect Pastor*, 35.
[11] Ibid., 96–97.

in another room. While you're at it, turn off all unnecessary notifications; it's hard to ignore a beeping, vibrating phone. You should also decide whether to give your cell number out, and if so, to whom.

When will you take appointments? Many pastors, including me, feel most productive when we schedule the mornings for study, preparation, and general admin while leaving meetings for the afternoon. This doesn't always work, but just as you watch your number of work nights, also watch how many meetings get scheduled outside of normal office hours.

It seems that it used to be more common for people to visit a pastor during the workday, much like we would expect to see a doctor. But this practice seems to be fading. Many of my appointments, if I let them, would gravitate toward times that are typically outside work hours, which means it's something I must watch closely.

Also, watch your eating. With so many evening meetings, it's easy to become unhealthy, as Gavin Ortlund points out:

> A pastor gets home from a difficult elder's meeting. It's nine o'clock in the evening, and it's been a long day. After a quick greeting to his wife, he beelines for the kitchen to reward himself from the burdens of the day by losing himself in Lay's potato chips, Red Vines licorice, and Dr. Pepper. Several hours later, he turns off the television and heads to bed. The stress is gone.[12]

What's wrong with this? Nothing, every once in a while. And if you ask me, it's fine if the Dr. Pepper is an IPA. But if candy and carbonation binges become the norm, you're not healthy; you're probably medicating something below the surface.

Speaking of health, remember "physical training is of some value" (1 Tim 4:8, NIV). Among its benefits, many pastors find exercise to be a good boundary marker; it's a stone wall that keeps work hours from getting out of hand. In the past, when I've been injured and unable to exercise, I tend to overwork.

In no way am I suggesting my boundaries should be yours. You must establish your own healthy patterns. Just keep in mind that

---

[12] Gavin Ortlund, "How to Fight Unhealthy Snacking: Dealing Well with Daily Depletion," *Desiring God*, July 7, 2015, http://www.desiringgod.org/articles/how-to-fight-unhealthy-snacking.

whatever boundaries you construct are there for your family, your fellow staff, your elders, and even your church members. It's hypocrisy to preach about our limits as humans and then to work as if these limits don't exist for you; our praxis should adorn preaching like a tie matching a shirt.

Again, the first hundred days might be a time to sprint; it helps to get the race off to a good start. But if you sprint, just know you're burning matches, and you only have a limited number. You don't want to be huffing and puffing for air before you've even crossed the first mile marker.

6. Lean on Friends and Mentors Outside the System

When you first arrive, especially if you're in a new city, you won't have many friends. I've found this to be tough and so has my wife. Before I was a pastor, whatever church we joined was something of a "third place"; it wasn't where I worked, nor was it where our extended family and neighbors were. But when you begin vocational ministry, the church becomes the center of your relational world. This can make for lonely Friday nights, especially for your spouse, who likely isn't meeting new people as regularly as you are.

Now, don't misunderstand me. Calling the church "work" doesn't mean you can't or shouldn't make friends there. You should. You must! But once you join staff, there's a hurdle that likely wasn't there when you were only a church member. Additionally, I've found that the more senior one's role at a church, the larger this hurdle of friendship becomes.

For all these reasons and more, it's important to cultivate your friendships as you transition. The same goes for mentors. They can be a kind, encouraging voice when you host a Christmas party that first year and only a few people come.

Most of all, don't lose heart. Building friendships takes time. You probably don't remember this, but those friendships you left behind took years to develop. As you meet people at church, keep your eyes open for front-runners—those few people who might become dear friends. You'll know when it happens. One evening you'll have dinner with others, and when you get home you'll think, *You know, that wasn't really work at all.* A friendship has begun.

7. Don't Spend All Your Time with Leaders

There's a certain wisdom to spending most of your day with the people who are most committed to your church's ministry. As I've said earlier, you should do this by taking fellow staff and elders out to dinner or coffee to spend time with them.

But I also encourage you to spend time with non-church leaders, with regular, run-of-the-mill Christians who are a part of your new church. Consider the example of Jesus. He had great crowds, the seventy-two, the twelve, and the three. He had his leaders, those who followed him and were closest to him. But he also spent time with the weak and the oppressed. He spent time with lepers, and they had his attention. Jesus expects the same pattern in his followers. Do you remember what he taught in Luke 14? Hear the words of Jesus on this point:

> When you give a dinner or a banquet, do not invite your friends or your brothers or your relatives or rich neighbors, lest they also invite you in return and you be repaid. But when you give a feast, invite the poor, the crippled, the lame, the blind, and you will be blessed, because they cannot repay you. For you will be repaid at the resurrection of the just. (Luke 14:12–14)

Obeying this might mean you meet with the elderly in your church to sing some old hymns and share cookies and coffee. It might mean hospital visits. It might mean grabbing another pastor on a Sunday after church to bring the Lord's Supper to a shut-in. If you lead the youth group, maybe you go out of your way to spend time with that kid who has no friends or a troubled home. When you begin a new pastorate, spend time with those who can never repay you, who seemingly have nothing to offer. It's absolutely worth it.

If you struggle with feeling like this won't help your church's ministry, or if you're wrestling with how much this will eat up your time, remember the words of Jesus: "For you will be repaid at the resurrection of the just."

8. Move with Your Family

There are situations when it's not the right choice to move with your family. Sometimes, the desire to let children finish their school year in a familiar place means a spouse must stay behind while you move to the new job. Sometimes you don't move with your family because of health challenges, perhaps because one of you must stay behind to care for a relative or parent. And sometimes, maybe often, it's the selling of a house that drives the decision.

But these situations should be weighed heavily against the opportunity cost. Beforehand, it can be difficult to imagine what it will cost to leave your family behind. Even if everything goes well and the situation only lasts a few months, bitterness can easily creep in toward the new church and even toward God.

And when I say move with your family, I don't just mean physically. It's possible to live in the same house with them but be a zombie. It's possible to be there physically while your mind and heart are elsewhere. Don't do this. Shut work down when you leave the office. When you come home, hide your phone and find your kids.

Author and pastor Robert Ramey confesses in his book *The Pastor's Start-up Manual*: "I nearly botched my entry into several parishes by simply being too eager to start working!" It wasn't that these congregations felt he was failing. He hit the ground burning matches. He failed because, as he puts it, "I was so anxious to begin my work that I neglected to help [my family] enter their new situation."[13]

Consider how Zack Eswine captures the inherent loneliness of a spouse during a move, especially one with a young family:

> When a couple enters ministry, the young love of ordinary life can get pressed out of them. She has often just given birth to a child. Or maybe they are newly married. But mostly they are already exhausted from their Bible-training pace, starting the work of ministry as those who already need a break. But to start work for God offers little time for residual fatigue. So the spouse goes with her ministry leader without roots to a new place with

---

[13] Ramey, *The Pastor's Start-up Manual*, 17.

a new child and a newer job. The church expects him to hit the ground running. He wants to show that he is worth their hire. He overworks all hours for the sake of Jesus while his new bride and newer baby try to learn to trust Jesus amid the dishwasher and *Sesame Street*, with no local friends and no firsthand knowledge of street names.[14]

You need to be there for your family, which means, if at all possible, you should move together.

9. Enjoy Your Honeymoon

I don't care much for using a real marriage as a metaphor for the marriage of a church and a pastor. But sometimes it does fit, even if in this case, a "ministry honeymoon" won't be as awesome as a marriage honeymoon. You didn't find a job as a chaplain at an all-inclusive resort in the Caribbean, did you?

Still, the two honeymoons share many things: a fresh start, new discoveries, and a steep learning curve. Try not to get overwhelmed. You'll never have this period of time in this place again. Enjoy it while it lasts.

*   *   *

"How to Involve Your Wife in Your Job Search"

By Kristen Wetherell

When my husband and I got married, he was pastoring the youth at our church. He loved his job and was excellent at it—but we knew the end was near. He had agreed to work in this role for five years with the hope of becoming a preaching pastor thereafter.

We hoped and prayed this would happen at the same local church, but only God knew.

Through many unknowns, we started discussing the possibilities. Would God somehow direct us to stay? Would he have us

---

[14] Eswine, *The Imperfect Pastor*, 41.

elsewhere near our home? Or would he call us to pick up everything and move across state lines?

After about a year of waiting, we got the call: We would be staying at the same church, in a different role. Hallelujah! But the waiting was intense, and it stretched and grew our marriage in a unique way.

Pastor, as you progress through your job search, know that your wife desires to be involved. She knows you better than anyone, will speak truthfully, and wants what's best for you. The following are five ways my husband involved me during our season of searching and waiting—and I hope they'll be helpful to you.

Through commitment. As husbands and wives are joined in the covenant of marriage and united in Christ, one spouse's calling means both spouses must be called. In other words, your wife should have peace and clarity about the jobs you're pursuing, especially when it comes to decision time. My husband always reminds me that "we're in this together." No, I may not be preaching on Sundays or pastoring the flock, but I'm one with him, so any job search needs to be a united effort and decision. Your devotion to your wife extends even to this.

Through prayer. All prayers should be prayed with fervency and faith, but during our year of waiting, prayers for a job were especially fervent. It's a sweet thing to come together with your wife to petition God for wisdom, direction, and job provision. As you see him faithfully move, even by degrees and in unexpected ways, you'll rejoice together and have great cause for thanksgiving, a lifeline of worship during hard and confusing seasons.

Through listening. Your wife will appreciate your ear. Waiting upon the Lord for such a vital thing as a job (no—a calling) can be taxing and emotional. You'll involve her and serve her well by listening to her process the journey and by valuing her input. Listen to what she's feeling and thinking, and know this speaks love to her.

Through sharing. Similarly, you'll appreciate your wife's listening ear, and she'll want to listen! Pursue open, consistent communication. Share your ideas, leads, and conversations. Tell her your hopes and prayers. I always valued my husband's intentionality to keep me in-the-loop with his thoughts and actions. It made me feel intimately involved.

Through rest. Finally, know when to stop and think on other things. Know when to pause the processing. Know when to end the topic of conversation and simply *enjoy*. Pausing to rest can be difficult when the pressure to find work is looming, but both of you will benefit from it. Burnout and frustration result from a lack of rest, but motivation and fruitfulness come when we heed this needful gift as couples. Marriage, too, is a gift from God—so enjoy it!

Proverbs 18:22 says, "He who finds a wife finds a good thing and obtains favor from the Lord." Amen, husbands! You're not alone in this. We're here to help, encourage, and uphold you, so give us the joy of being involved as you pursue God's calling upon your life.

Kristen Wetherell is the coauthor of *Hope When It Hurts*, a Bible teacher, and the former content manager at Unlocking the Bible. She and her husband, Brad, are members of The Orchard in Itasca, Illinois, where Brad is a campus pastor.

OVERFLOW WITH GRATITUDE

I will give thanks to the Lord with my whole heart;
I will recount all of your wonderful deeds.
– Psalm 9:1

A huge part of finishing well is saying "thank you" a lot. Even before you get your new job, you should be practicing this final tip. Why? Because from the very beginning of the job-search process, and especially near the end, you should overflow with gratitude.

From Beginning to End, Overflow with Gratitude

This relates to our earlier discussion of how to build and leverage your personal network. People don't want to be in your network if they suspect you're using them every time you contact them. A sure way to make people feel used, and indeed to actually use them, is to never thank them.

If you want people to feel used, let them help you get a job. Let them pray for you. Let them make personal requests of their circle of friends. Let them proofread your cover letters. Let them give an hour of their time to serve as a reference. Let them write recommendation letters, and let them coach you through the interview process.

And then finally, after all that, never say thank you. That's how you use people. That's how you get grease everywhere. Don't do this.

The right way to say thank you will depend on who the person is and what they did for you. A passive recipient of your stock email isn't on the same level as your current senior pastor who happily served as one of your references even though, deep down, he didn't want you to leave.

In saying thank you, you should do more than send an e-mail blast or post something on Facebook. You should write a letter to people *by hand*. For others, you should perhaps do even more. This is certainly true of your spouse. She loves you and prays for you and gave you a hug when four churches said no. She put the kids to bed while you lived in the library looking for a job. Now it's time to take her on a date—a nice one! Buy flowers and celebrate together.

Let's take this just a bit further. If we express thanksgiving toward people, then how much more ought we overflow with gratitude to God. After all, it's God who's been working behind the scenes every step of the way. As James says, "Every good gift and every perfect gift is from above" (1:17). Consider how Paul expresses his thanksgiving to God:

I thank my God in all my remembrance of you. (Phil 1:3)

We always thank God, the Father of our Lord Jesus Christ, when we pray for you. (Col 1:3)

We give thanks to God always for all of you, constantly mentioning you in our prayers, remembering before our God and Father your work of faith and labor of love and steadfastness of hope in our Lord Jesus Christ. (1 Thess 1:2–3)

True gratitude traces blessings back to their ultimate source. This is why true gratitude is always oriented toward God. We see this kind of gratitude in many of the psalms. Psalm 136 is a classic example. It has twenty-six verses, and each verse has a unique statement expressing thanksgiving to God, which is then followed by the repetition of the line "for his steadfast love endures forever."

The psalm starts with God.

Give thanks to the LORD, *for he is good,*
for his steadfast love endures forever.
Give thanks to the God of gods,
for his steadfast love endures forever.
Give thanks to the LORD *of lords,*
for his steadfast love endures forever. (vv. 1–3)

The psalm ends with God.

Give thanks to the God of heaven,
for his steadfast love endures forever. (v. 26)

In the middle of the psalm there's thanksgiving to God for general things.

[It is] he who gives food to all flesh,
for his steadfast love endures forever. (v. 25)

But not just for general things. The psalm *also* thanks God for specific things.

[He] overthrew Pharaoh and his host in the Red Sea,
for his steadfast love endures forever. (v. 15)

This is Godward gratitude. It starts with God, it ends with God, and along the way it sees every blessing as a gracious gift from a gracious God.

We could keep going, but the point is clear. Our gratitude should ultimately culminate on God. But if we're honest, sometimes we're not very good at this. Often when we need help from God, we spend lots of time praying on the front end: *Lord, help me preach a sermon that honors you, is faithful to the text, and presents the gospel in a clear and compelling way.* But we spend far too little time praying on the back end: *Hmmm, church is over. What's for lunch?*

A Story of Thanksgiving

Let me end with a story. When I was first looking for a job after seminary, it wasn't going very well. I'd started looking nine months before graduation. This seemed like enough time, but in my case nothing was panning out.

At the beginning, one of my first tasks was making a list of things that would constitute my dream job. I listed things *about the church*: size, denomination, theology, and family involvement. I listed things *about the job*: how often I'd preach, how much administration it would entail, and what salary would provide for our needs. I listed things *about the location*: the size, the amenities (is there a Target and a Chipotle?), the demographics (is it a college town?), and the weather (is it warm?).

I didn't do this because I felt my first job out of seminary would or even should be my dream job. I knew better than that. Really, I just wanted to figure out how God had wired me and to understand what I would be qualified for, what I would enjoy, and where my family would thrive.

But this was all happening not long after the economic crash of 2008. Churches simply weren't hiring. I've learned many had similar experiences during these years. If a church had three pastors and one left, they were learning to get by with two. And if a church was growing and needed to add staff, they weren't.

I understood this. After all, it's difficult to ask the congregation to keep giving, perhaps even to increase their giving, when you know many in the church have lost their jobs.

At some point in this search process I remember saying to my wife, "You know that list we made, the one with our dream job in the dream city? I'm throwing it in the trash. I just need to find a job—forget the *right* job."

Why do I bring this up? Well, eventually, I did get a job as a pastor in a local church, and a few months after I started, I realized something: that list I made of the perfect job in the perfect city, well, I didn't get it.

Instead, I got something better.

The church wasn't perfect, but it was *perfect for me*—even in all its flaws. The church was a perfect place for me to learn and struggle and grow. It was the perfect place to develop my gifts, which admittedly were very raw. It was a perfect place to give and receive love.

For this, even though I no longer serve that church, I am forever thankful—thankful both to that church for taking a chance on me and to God for leading me in their direction.

I hope and pray that when you've found your next job, God will cause you to feel the same.

APPENDICES

DON'T
Just
SEND A
RESUME

JOB-SEARCH CHECKLIST

Introduction: Set the Proper Foundation

____ **Don't reinvent yourself; re-identify with Christ.** Culture celebrates becoming whoever you want to be. This reinventing, however, is often done in an idolatrous way. God gives us major life transitions not for personal reinvention but rather to re-identify with who we are in Christ.

____ **Pray without ceasing.** There's so much to do when looking for a job. If you don't commit to pray, you won't. You'll just work and work and work. Stop. Sharpen the axe. There's a forest up ahead.

____ **Trust in the goodness and sovereignty of God.** The job search can be a roller coaster. Of course, you should do your best to mitigate risk, but how will you know if a church is right? You can't know, at least not entirely. But what you can do—what you must do—is trust in the goodness and sovereignty of God.

____ **Know whether it's time for a transition.** Before you move, you need to know whether you *should* move. Try not to get near-sighted about this. Don't let a few annoyances sour you. Instead, listen to your passions, think with your brain, consult those you trust, and above all seek the Lord.

Part I: Smoking the Curve

Chapter 1: Write Custom Cover Letters and Resumes

____ **Always include a short, custom cover letter.** It's easy to send an e-mail and simply attach a resume. But don't. Easy won't make you stand out. Invest the time and do it right. Create a professional, custom cover letter for each church.

____ **Choose the right resume style for you.** There are many ways to lay out a resume. Most of the differences are merely artistic, but some are structural. You need to make sure you choose the resume structure that's right for you, whether a business style or a skill-based style.

Chapter 2: Correspond like a Professional

____ **With sermon audio and video samples, suggest a few of the best but give them several.** It's hard to know how much to send to churches. Early in the process, just give them your best two samples. Later in the process, you can give them more.

____ **Include high-quality pictures and a family bio.** Most candidates don't do this. Churches, however, find it very helpful to have a quality picture and a family bio. And if you do this well, you'll stand out from the crowd.

____ **Select quality and diverse references.** Employers expect your references to sing your praises. Make sure you select quality, diverse references so you don't disappoint.

____ **Consider sending a recommendation letter.** If John Piper will not write a recommendation letter for you, you can still have a meaningful letter if you get one from the right person.

____ **Use simple, professional formatting.** Receiving a resume using six different fonts is a deal breaker. If you send a resume that doesn't use professional formatting, churches won't care if you have memorized the Greek New Testament.

____ **Only send PDFs (not Microsoft Word documents).** Make sure the hard work you did to make a professional document isn't garbled by different versions of Microsoft Word or equivalent programs.

____ **Send only one attachment.** It's very easy to accidentally misplace multiple attachments. You worked hard on your resume packet. Make sure it stays together.

Chapter 3: Gain the Legit Factor

____ **Send communication from your personal e-mail account.** If you send communication from either your current employer or school e-mail, you may lose stuff you'll potentially want to save. Instead, use a professional but personal e-mail account.

____ **Keep track of everything.** If you start talking to multiple churches, the details will get foggy. Keep track of everything so you don't call Pastor Steve, Pastor Stephen—or was it Stephen, not Steve?

____ **If you are in a different country, work extra hard.** There are significant hurdles to applying for a job while living in a different country, but there are several things you can do to make the leap smaller.

____ **Make the follow-up phone call.** After you send your cover letter and resume, you just wait for them to e-mail or call, right? No way. Not if you're really interested in the job. Pick up the phone and tell them.

____ **Stay positive regarding previous job transitions.** We all have a tale of woe. Save it for another day. Stay positive early on.

____ **Know whom, when, and in what order to tell people you are taking a new job.** You don't want to mess up the communication of your departure. Tell the right people in the right order at the right time.

____ **Gain the legit factor.** The legit factor means people believe your life not only displays the gifting of the Spirit but also the fruit of the Spirit. Therefore, the first priority of your life is to be legit—forget appearances. Work to have character made of gold, not iron pyrite, and strive to show this to your hopeful employer. Do this through your personal network, references, recommendation letters, and all-around integrity.

Chapter 4: Network and Search for Openings

___ **Build and leverage your personal network.** If you want a job, knowing how to network in a godly and efficient manner will help a lot.

___ **Be intentional on your social media, blog, and website.** The first thing an employer will do when they become interested in you is search your name on the Internet. What are they going to find on your Facebook page or Twitter account?

___ **Know where to find job openings.** Once you've put on your running shoes and gym shorts, you're ready to run the race. Now you must find your way to the starting line.

Part II: Making the Move

Chapter 5: Understand the Hiring Process

___ **Know how a church will hire you.** Often, the hiring process is far more bewildering than it should be. Sometimes the church is confused, sometimes the candidate is confused, and sometimes they both are. As much as it depends on you, make sure you know what's going on every step of the way.

Chapter 6: Over-Prepare for Interviews

___ **Over-prepare for job interviews.** If you don't over-prepare, then you are under-prepared, and under-prepared candidates don't get hired.

___ **Learn names to make a personal connection.** It's so nice to have someone remember your name. Just as the Good Shepherd knows the names of his sheep, so should you work to learn names. It's a skill that improves with practice.

___ **Have a mock interview.** You're probably not as good at interviewing as you think you are. And even if you are good at it, why not get better?

Chapter 7: Evaluate the Transplant Criteria

____ **Evaluate all the pastoral transplant criteria.** There are many things to think about when considering what will make a new church a good match for you and your family. The wise candidate will evaluate all of them.

Chapter 8: Ask Lots of Questions

____ **Ask lots and lots of questions.** The church isn't the only one doing the interviewing. You're also interviewing them. Act like it. The church will appreciate it because it shows you're thoughtful (not desperate) and interested (not aloof).

____ **Speak to former employees.** Talking to former employees can be helpful but tricky. If you do it, know what to ask and how to ask it.

____ **Send more samples of your work.** You impressed the church with your professional cover letter, resume, and a limited sample of your work. Now it's time to send them a little more.

____ **Know when to play the field and when to narrow the search.** What if two or three churches all seem to like you *at the same time*? And what if you like them? This might be okay, but at some point you must narrow the search.

____ **Don't get desperate.** Don't sacrifice your principles when your prospects seem bleak. Don't accept a call to a toxic church just to pay your bills. There are other ways to make ends meet.

____ **Be gracious when you tell them "no."** Invariably, during your career you'll be offered a job that isn't right, and you'll have to turn it down. When you tell them no, do so graciously. That's how you want churches to treat you.

____ **Prepare your family.** If *you* are ready to move, that's great. But you won't have a healthy ministry over the long haul if your home life is a wreck. Your spouse and family come first, not the church. Spend the time and energy to prepare your family to move, not only on the physical side but the emotional side as well.

Chapter 9: Talk about Money

____ **Don't be shy or afraid to talk about money.** Like networking, talking about money is often considered taboo. But it shouldn't be. Godly people can talk about money in godly ways.

Part III: Finishing the Race

Chapter 10: Finish Strong

____ **Before you leave, finish like a champ.** It's so easy to coast to the finish line. That's not what Christians are meant to do. Christians run to the end, maybe even sprint.

Chapter 11: Restart Strong

____ **In your first 100 days, start strong all over again.** You don't have to build Rome in a day—or one hundred days. But you do need to think about the things you want to happen over your pastoral tenure and how to begin working toward them from the get-go.

Chapter 12: Overflow with Gratitude

____ **From beginning to end, overflow with gratitude.** It is nothing short of ungodly to climb over others as you transition to a new job. It's godly to gush with gratitude. Be godly, and be grateful.

131 QUESTIONS TO ASK A POTENTIAL EMPLOYER

One of the best things you can do in the job-search process is ask questions. I have created some of the questions below from scratch and others I've adapted. I've organized them by categories so they're easier to use.

Before you read them, here are a few things to keep in mind. First, the questions are malleable. Some questions may not fit your context until you tweak them.

Second—and I want to stress this—the goal isn't to ask every question. That would be painful for both church and candidate. The goal is to ask questions that seem appropriate for the stage of the process you're in. Early on, you might ask questions like, "What are some hobbies among the staff?" or "What are the expectations for a pastor's spouse?" Then, later in the process, you might ask about putting the compensation package into writing. If you switch the order, at best you could seem cold and insensitive. At worst, you might not make it to the next round where you could have asked more difficult questions.

Finally, as you look at the list, keep in mind certain questions must be addressed to certain people. Some questions are better for the search committee, some for other staff members, some for people in the congregation, and some for the elders. For example, in a meeting with the current staff, don't ask if someone on staff needs to be terminated. However, if you're interviewing for the role of senior pastor, it's a question you might privately ask the elders near the end of the process.

General

1. Can you give me a brief history of the church?
2. How long have you been planning to fill this position?
3. What are the circumstances that created the need for this role?
4. What is the sequence and timeline of the hiring process?
5. When do you expect to call references?
6. When do you hope to have someone in place?
7. How many candidates are still in the running?
8. As I read the job description, I'm wondering how much time you expect to be allotted to the various items listed. Could you help me understand what a typical week might look like?
9. If I am called to your church, what sort of things would make you say, "Wow, this is a great fit" after a year or so?
10. What, if anything, made my resume/application stand out? Why do you think I will help this church?
11. In what ways, if at all, do you think my age might affect my reception both in the church and among the leadership?
12. May I have an unofficial visit to your church to see what things are like before the official interview/candidating weekend?
13. Your website states _____. What does that mean?
14. How does a person move from random attender at your church, to member, and then to leader?
15. If exciting things were happening at your church (and they likely are), what would they be?
16. What are some of the hobbies of the other staff? What do you do for fun?
17. Do you regularly take staff and/or elder retreats? What are they like?

18. May I have a copy of a recent newsletter? Church bulletin? Financial statement? Congregational meeting minutes?
19. Does your church have a policy manual? May I have a copy?
20. Can you please describe your worship style?
21. How would you evaluate a successful worship service?
22. What qualities did you appreciate about the person who had this role previously?
23. In which ways are you similar to other churches in your community? In which ways are you different?
24. Generally speaking, do you think people in the community have a positive or negative view of your church?
25. Which ministries in your church seem to be most successful? Why?
26. When did the most recent round of new members join?
27. How many members do you have vs. how many people attend regularly each week?
28. When was the last time the membership rolls were pruned of people who no longer attend?
29. What do visitors often comment on?
30. Who is responsible for putting together the order of service?
31. Who is responsible for the website?
32. Does your church have expectations for pastors regarding social media?
33. This is hard to predict, but approximately how many weddings and funerals might the pastor be expected to officiate in the next year?
34. What missionaries and parachurch organizations does your church support?

Theology and Practice

35. What is the church government structure?
36. Does the church have a statement of faith? How was it created?
37. Is your statement of faith ever re-worked? If so, what is the process?

38. Does your church have an official position on the end times? God's sovereignty and human responsibility? The charismatic spiritual gifts? The age of the earth? Alcohol? Divorce and remarriage?

39. What is the church's view of male and female roles?

40. How is baptism practiced at your church (frequency and format, who leads, who can participate)?

41. How is communion practiced at your church (frequency and format, who leads, who can participate)?

42. Are you open to making changes to how baptism and communion are practiced?

43. Let's say I move here, and my neighbor wants to check out our church. He is gay. What will his experience be like? Or what would you hope it to be?

44. Does your church have a favorite Bible translation? Do you prefer one to preach from?

45. How do you prefer to preach/teach the Bible: expositionally, topically, book studies, another method?

46. If a pastor at your church was asked to officiate a wedding, can you see him ever saying no? What circumstances might bring that about?

47. What doctrines excite the leaders of your church? What doctrines do you prefer to avoid?

48. How would you counsel a person who accepts Christ but remains in a sinful lifestyle?

49. Are there particular authors and pastors you admire? Who?

50. What theological trends, broadly speaking, create concern among your church and leaders?

51. How much should a pastor address political issues?

52. Does your church have a history of endorsing candidates and political parties?

53. How many Sundays would you expect me to preach each year? [Worship and youth pastors can ask something different but related.]

54. Can you provide me a list of songs your church has sung in the last month? What are some of your church's favorites?

55. If someone were to show up to the church office asking for gas money to get home (or to make some other benevolence request), how is this request processed?

56. Have all your teachers read and agreed to teach in concert with your doctrinal statement?

Church Health and Planning

57. May I please have a copy of the annual budget and some information on monthly giving from the last year?

58. During this recent change of pastors, has a self-study been done by the church, either formally or informally? If so, may I please see the results?

59. Did the leadership of the church conduct an exit interview with the previous staff member who did this job? If so, may I see notes from the interview?

60. Are internal candidates being considered for this role? If so, who?

61. Do you have a small-group ministry? If so, how many people are currently in small groups? What percentage of the church is this?

62. If it were decided more people could be reached for Christ by changing the name of the church, would you be open to that?

63. Do you own your church building/property?

64. Is there adequate funding in the church budget for your leaders and staff to accomplish the tasks placed before them?

65. Where do you see the Spirit of God working in your church?

66. Are there regular times of prayer among the staff?

67. What mechanisms are in place to help the staff avoid burnout?

68. What are the demographics of your church?

69. How reflective are your church demographics of the local community?

70. If your church continued to grow for the next five years, what changes do you anticipate?

71.   Regarding ministry style, can you give an illustration of another church you are trying to model your church after?

72.   What ways do you see teamwork taking place among the staff?

73.   In which areas would you say your church is understaffed?

74.   How long have the other employees worked here?

75.   Besides calling a pastor, what other items are top priorities in the next year?

76.   Has the interim period been healing? In what ways?

77.   Could you tell me about other healthy churches nearby? Describe your relationship with them.

Facilities and Property[1]

78.   Are the church facilities in good shape? Is there any work to the building that needs to be done right away?

79.   What is the seating capacity of the sanctuary?

80.   Is there adequate office space? Classroom space?

81.   What is (or would be) a limiting factor in church growth (e.g., parking, office space, sanctuary size, children's classrooms)?

82.   What is the community like around your church (e.g., commercial, industrial, residential, rural, urban)?

83.   Do many people from the surrounding community attend your church?

84.   How far does the typical churchgoer have to drive to get to your church?

85.   Have there been any construction projects (upkeep or expansion) that have been put on hold? If so, why? Are there plans or hopes to do this work in the future?

86.   Does the church owe money on the property? If so, how much? What convictions does the church have about debt?[2]

---

[1] Some of these questions have been adapted from Umidi, *Confirming the Pastoral Call*, 127.

[2] Asking this question about church debt and evaluating the answer are two different things. If you do not have the education and ability to discern what is an acceptable and unacceptable amount of debt (and savings), consult with someone who can help you get clarity about financial matters. As a general rule, one author notes that unhealthy church debt occurs when total church debt exceeds three times the annual budget (Page, *Looking for a New Pastor*, 27).

Leadership, Structure, and Conflict

87. In what areas was the previous pastor specifically gifted? What areas were more of a challenge?

88. What has been the most controversial thing in your church during the last year?

89. What issues have regularly caused friction in this church? Among staff? Among the elder board?

90. Do you have weekly staff meetings? If so, what do they look like?

91. Do accurate job descriptions exist for each staff member? May I see them?

92. What is your church polity? Are there elders, deacons, ministry leaders, etc.? How do they relate to each other?

93. From the perspective of authority and structure, what is the relationship of a staff pastor to the elder board and congregation?

94. Does your church have an organizational chart? If so, may I see it? Could you explain the relationships to me?

95. Is this church affiliated with a larger movement or denomination? If not, what are some means and methods to cultivate healthy, structural accountability?

96. To what extent are the non-staff elders involved in the planning of sermons and sermon series?

97. Can you recount a time of church conflict that resulted in a form of discipline?

98. Which current leaders in your church, staff or non-staff, are considered indispensable? Why? Have you had to let someone go in the last ten years? If so, what were the circumstances?

99. Have any former staff members left ministry altogether?

100. What happened to the previous pastor or staff person in this role? What were the circumstances for their departure? May I contact them? What are they doing now?

101. If you could go back and change how a situation was handled in the last year, what would it be and why? What would you do differently?

102. Are there issues among the current staff that will need to be addressed once the new hire arrives? Are there even staff members who may need to be terminated by the new hire?
103. How is the annual budget prepared and approved?
104. Who is responsible for keeping spending in line with the budget?
105. Do you have any divorced persons in leadership? Can you tell me more about the church's view on this?

Family

106. What are the expectations for my spouse?
107. What roles do the spouses of other staff at the church play?
108. What are the expectations for my children?
109. How many nights a week do you expect the person you hire to have work commitments outside the home?
110. If my children were to attend a youth group at a neighboring church, would that be a problem?
111. If I had a Christmas party (with neighbors, friends, and church people) and alcohol was served, would that be an issue?
112. Among families with children, is there a mode of education that is most common (public school, homeschool, private school, Christian school)?
113. Are there any expectations regarding education of our children?
114. Is there a certain proximity to the church, spoken or unspoken, in which the pastor should live?

Money and Job-Performance Reviews

115. On which days of the week is the new employee expected to be in the office?
116. Is there an openness to doing some work remotely?
117. Do you conduct performance reviews at the end of each year? If so, what do they look like? And who does them?

118. Can you please write up the salary package, including things like health, life, and disability insurance; health savings account; continuing education and conference money; funds for ministry tools such as books and computer software; cell phone; moving expenses; paid holidays; vacation; etc.? (For full list see chapter 9, section "Components of a Salary Package.")

119. Is there a church parsonage? If the candidate desired not to use it, would compensation be adjusted accordingly?

120. If in three years I felt called to pursue an advanced degree (e.g., D.Min.), how would that be received? What support, if any, could I expect from the church?

121. Does your church have a sabbatical policy? If so, what is it? If not, would you be open to creating one?

122. Does the congregation have a policy of reviewing the pastor's salary package each year?

123. How will success be measured, formally and informally? By whom? How often?

124. If I must move to take this position, what, if any, moving costs are covered?

125. What are the time expectations in the areas of preaching/teaching, counseling, visitation, and office hours?

126. Is there any allowance for a pastor to preach/teach off site, whether at another church, conference, seminary, or elsewhere?

127. If a pastor preaches off site, what support do you offer (e.g., help with travel expenses, time to work on messages)?

128. How accessible are pastoral salaries to the congregation? Are salaries printed in weekly, monthly, or yearly budgets, or are they only made available to a select group of leaders? Would your church be open to discussing changes to this policy?

129. If you are not pursuing employment with a church but another Christian organization, consider asking this: Will this employee qualify for the IRS housing allowance available to ministers? (The answer will depend on a number of factors,

including the specifics of the organization and the employee's role within it.[3])

130. Is there a severance policy? If so, what is it?
131. Do you have a policy or opinion on who owns the material produced by pastors (sermons, curriculum, etc.) while employed with you? Would you be open to a discussion about it?

---

[3] See Rainer, *The Minister's Salary*, 96–99.

Benjamin and his wife Brooke have six children. Benjamin enjoys reading, wrestling with his children, dating his wife, eating at Chipotle, and riding his bicycle in the early hours of the morning.

He earned a degree in mechanical engineering from the University of Missouri and a masters of divinity from Covenant Theological Seminary in St. Louis, Missouri. He is a teaching pastor at Community Evangelical Free Church in Harrisburg, PA. He is coauthor of *More People to Love* and author of *Struggle Against Porn*. He has also written for *The Gospel Coalition*, *Desiring God*, and *For The Church*.

If you would like to read more from Benjamin Vrbicek, please subscribe to his blog, BenjaminVrbicek.com, where he writes a weekly post, or e-mail him at Benjamin@fanandflame.com. He'd love to hear from you, especially if you'd like coaching during a job transition.